Jimmy Young

Jimmy Young

MICHAEL JOSEPH/RAINBIRD

For Alicia

First published in Great Britain in 1982 by
Michael Joseph Limited
44 Bedford Square, London WC1 and
The Rainbird Publishing Group Limited
40 Park Street, London W1Y 4DE
who designed and produced the book

ISBN 0 7181 2142 2

Filmset by Input Typesetting Limited, London
Origination by Lithospeed Limited, London
Printed and bound by Mackays of Chatham Limited, Chatham, Kent

Contents

Acknowledgments

The author and publishers are grateful to the following for permission to reproduce photographs on the pages indicated: *Ariel* 115 *bottom*; Associated Newspapers 52, 56 *top*, 113 *top*, 119 *top*, 119 *bottom left*, 121 *top*; Associated Press 114; BBC 49 *top*, 50, 58 *top*, 64 *top right*, 115 *top*, 116 *bottom*, 123 *bottom*, 126 *bottom*; BBC Hulton Picture Library 55; Laurence Burns 62; Central Press Photos 53 *bottom*, 56 *bottom*; The *Daily Telegraph* photo by Tony Marshal 54; Express Newspapers 51, cartoons by Jak: 64 *bottom right*, 113 *bottom*; Barry Hopkins/Capricorn Video Services 61 *top left*; *Illustrated London News Picture Library* 126 *top*, 128; Keystone 53 *top*, 121 *bottom*; London Weekend Television 64 *top left*; Doug Mckenzie Photographic Services Ltd 63 *bottom*; Punch/David Langdon 119 *bottom right*; *Radio Times* photo by Don Smith 63 *top*, photo by Ric Gemmell 124; Press Association 49 *bottom*, 58 *bottom*, 59, 117, 118, 120, 125, 127; Thames Television 122, 123 *top*; W H Thomas 61 *bottom*; Percy Thrower 64 *bottom left*; Universal Pictorial Press 57; *Woman's Own* 61 *top right*; Jimmy Young 60.

1-The Beginnings

The date was 4 December 1979 and I was late for lunch. As a matter of fact, I was *very* late for lunch. What made it even worse was that it was a lunch in my honour, and my hosts were some of the BBC's 'top brass'. Still, not to worry. I had a pretty fair opening line: 'Terribly sorry to be late,' I'd say, 'but I was delayed at Buckingham Palace.'

I had been to the Palace to collect my O.B.E. The gong had come to me completely out of the blue in the Queen's Birthday Honours List. Some newspapers said it was because I was the new Prime Minister Mrs Thatcher's 'favourite interviewer' although as far as I know she has never said so. Anyway, for whatever reason, as requested I presented myself at Buck House at 10 a.m. to be 'gonged' by the Queen. The Beeb had kindly decided to mark the occasion by laying on a luncheon for me afterwards. Unfortunately, and unusually for the BBC, their timing was somewhat less than perfect. The lunch invitation said 12.30 for 1 p.m. I protested that the investiture was unlikely to be over before 12.30, but to no avail. So, at 12.30 there I was having press pictures taken in the Palace yard, followed by an interview for BBC Television News. I finally left the Palace at 12.50 to enter a huge traffic jam. Small wonder then that it was 1.15 p.m. before I reached Broadcasting House, to be confronted by the news that my producer, executive producer and the head of Radio 2 had been on the office phone since 12.45 trying to find out where the hell I was!

The lunch was being held in the Governors' dining-room, which I entered at 1.30 p.m. Now the Governors' dining-room is ruled not, as you might imagine, by the Governors, but by Mrs Kitty Smith. Ruled, I may say, with a firm manner, and a smashing smile. As I entered, it was only too apparent that Mrs Smith, B.E.M., was worried that her lunch was going to be spoiled. However, after an apology to Kitty and the top brass, in that order, all was fine.

Very well, you may say, so it was a big day for Jimmy Young, but why start the book with it? The reason is simple. I start the book with it because it was *it* which started the book.

Douglas Muggeridge, then Director of Programmes Radio, hosted the lunch. At the end of it he made a speech and very flattering it was. He referred to 'this unique programme; there is not a similar current affairs vehicle in either Europe or the United States of America' and he made my ears burn by speaking of 'this unique broadcaster who has completely changed the face of the presentation of current affairs within the BBC.'

It was the end of the speech which told me I must begin work. Douglas turned to me and said, 'Jimmy, over the weekend I was re-reading your autobiography which you published in 1973. I again enjoyed every word of it. But you have a better book inside you now because of the places to which you have travelled, the people you have met, and the whole area of current affairs which you have explored. I tell you again, as I've told you for the last two years. Get down to it and write the damned thing.'

This is it.

By the beginning of 1973 I had already had three separate careers: night club pianist and bandleader in the early Fifties; pop singer with number one hits in 'Too Young', 'Unchained Melody' and 'The Man From Laramie' in the mid-Fifties; disc jockey with the BBC and Radio Luxembourg in the Sixties. I never dreamed that 1973 would give me the greatest opportunity of all.

For years I had been convinced that the average man and woman were passionately interested in what went on in the world around them, and that they were frustrated in their search for knowledge by the élitist style of many news and current affairs programmes. I longed for the opportunity to develop a completely new approach to this whole area of broadcasting. My opportunity to do just this came about in the oddest way. I was still a disc jockey on Radio 1 when I was summoned by the then Managing Director Radio, Mr (now Sir Ian) Trethowan.

'Sit down and have a drink', he said and poured me a large gin and tonic. This is always a dodgy moment at the BBC. It *can* mean pat-on-the-back-time. It can also mean just the opposite. Judging by Ian's opening remark it looked as though it would be 'just the opposite'. 'Looking at your work I reckon we're getting about forty per cent effort from you', continued Ian.

'I don't know what you're talking about, Ian', said I.

'Yes you do', he said; 'You put the records on, then sit back and read the paper.' It was true. I owned up.

'So, why don't you move to Radio 2 and do some *real* broadcasting?' he asked.

'What kind of programme do you want me to do?' I countered. Out popped the line which was to change my life.

'What I want you to do isn't important,' Ian said; 'what's important is what sort of broadcasting *you* want to do.' It was now or never. I took a deep breath.

I said, 'I would like to be free to talk to anyone, anywhere, about anything, as long as my gut feeling tells me it will interest my listeners. And if that means interviews with the Prime Minister, the Chancellor of the Exchequer or the Head of British Rail, so be it.'

To my amazement Ian said, 'I'm sold.' He went on, 'Go and talk to Douglas about it. If you can sell him the idea as you've sold me, you're on.'

And that is how Douglas Muggeridge, my host on 4 December 1979, Ian Trethowan and I, set up the programme which I hoped would open up to a much wider audience the often mysterious and remote world of politics and current affairs.

My last Radio 1 programme on 29 June 1973 was a bitter-sweet occasion. My studio was packed with friends: Head of Radio 1, Derek Chinnery; my dear friend, and producer for many years, Doreen Davies; Paul Williams, also a 'JY Prog' producer; Teddy Warrick; Tony Blackburn and many others with whom I had worked. The farewell champagne flowed. So, very nearly, did a few tears. Then, suddenly, my closing signature tune ended and I was alone with the realization that I had taken a tremendous decision. My future career as a broadcaster, if I had one, depended on whether I could make this new kind of broadcasting work.

I told myself I must not think negatively. I must think, instead, of how to interest and involve people in areas and events often considered too boring or serious for Radio 2. Think, I told myself, about communicating with people. That is what *you* are all about, and this is your chance really to prove it. And so, on 2 July, the great experiment began.

Nervous, very conscious that many eyes in the BBC were on me, I moved to Radio 2 and the start of my fourth career. By coincidence BBC Television were, at the time, filming a forty-five-minute documentary about me, called 'The World of Jimmy Young'. Michael Darlow, in charge of the television production, had decided, quite naturally, that the first day of my new job would make a super end to his film. I couldn't, and didn't, complain at his enthusiasm, but, as you can well imagine, a studio full of lights, cameras, camera crews and television production staff was just about all I needed on Day One of my Radio 2 programme.

However, luck was with me. The first person I interviewed on Radio 2 was courageous, gutsy, gritty Erin Pizzey. She's outspoken. She's a fighter; and you probably won't need me to tell you that she founded the Chiswick Women's Aid Hostel in London, for battered wives. Erin is an enthusiast and enthusiasm is infectious. In no time, I became so absorbed that I stopped doing 'an interview' and became involved in 'a conversation'. I didn't realize it at the time, of course, but this was actually my natural style. It was by 'getting involved', not just asking questions parrot fashion, that I was going to be able to extract so much information and so many interesting opinions from the people to whom I talked.

Perhaps I should explain in a little more detail how our programme differed from existing ones. First of all I should emphasize that, like all current affairs programmes, the 'Jimmy Young Programme' is the result of the hard work of a highly experienced and efficient team. We have two producers, a chief, and assistant chief researcher, plus a back-up research team. There is a production secretary in the studio, and other secretaries working in the offices. When we are not actually in the studio broadcasting, the programme operates from five adjoining offices on the second floor of Broadcasting House. These, you might say, are 'campaign headquarters'.

It is in other areas where the differences, and they are marked, occur. Current affairs programmes do not, as a rule, use music. We do. When we began in 1973 some of our competitors seized on this fact. They said it 'trivialized' current affairs. I knew it didn't. Quite the opposite: music is one of the programme's great advantages. From the beginning I realized it would give me the opportunity to run much longer interviews: a break for a couple of minutes of 'palate-cleansing music', then back to the discussion again.

It took a few years for some current affairs folk to cotton on to the strength of the format. When they did, we were, of course, much imitated.

Another very important element in the programme, indeed perhaps the most important, is the listeners' response. Although we are not, officially, a 'phone-in' programme I have never actively *discouraged* our listeners from phoning in. Don't ask me how they discover the number to ring because I never broadcast a telephone number. The fact is though that they do. Not only in Britain either, but in Scandinavia and on the Continent as well. Therefore we get almost immediate comment or 'reaction' as I call it on whatever is being said. It's rather like a continuous, daily referendum of our audience. I think it is one of the most immediate, and exciting parts of the programme. Sometimes it gets a bit *too* exciting and then we have to apologize to the BBC switchboard ladies. They're very good and understanding with us though, and it's an aspect of the programme which I would hate to be without.

Our method of working in the studio also differs greatly from the conventional. Broadcasting studios, broadly speaking, divide into two categories. 'Self-operated', which mine is, and 'non self-operated', which almost all other current affairs studios are. In a 'non self-operated studio' the presenter merely sits in front of the microphone and chats, while engineers take care of the mechanics. In a 'self-operated studio' the presenter does the lot!

So, in my studio, in addition to interviewing up to three guests at any one time, I personally operate two microphones, three record turntables, three tape channels, and three cassette players. It sounds complicated, and it is, but it does mean I have complete control and can be very flexible.

Because of the way it originated we have, for a current affairs programme, an unusual structure. For instance, I have no editor or assistant editor. The team, at shop floor level, is what the JY Prog is all about, and our unconventional approach, while no doubt not suitable for every programme, has certainly paid off for us. My producer, two chief researchers, production secretary and I run the programme, with consistent and ever present back-up from all the other members of the team. Once we have decided what subjects we are going to cover, the clock in my head, and my gut feeling, take over. It is these two factors alone which make me decide when to break for music. Or indeed, whether there is a need to break at all. I can decide, *in the studio*, whether to drop an item and cover, live, some important event just happening on the other side of the world. And it is 'self-operating', difficult and arduous though it is, which helps give us the edge.

Most current affairs programmes record their interviews in advance. They then edit and transmit them. In almost complete contrast, unless we are absolutely forced to, we record nothing. We even managed, against all the odds, to do it this way from Moscow. And Egypt, Israel, Zimbabwe and Tokyo.

I hope this will have given you some idea of what the atmosphere is like in the studio called, Jimmy Young Continuity 'D'. It's instant. It's live. It's certainly exciting. In my opinion, and all of us on the team, it's what broadcasting in the 1980s is all about.

However, back in 1973, all that was on my mind was survival.

2-Politicians are Human

There were many battles to be fought, many near disasters before the 'JY Prog' could be called an unqualified success. I finished the first programme in 1973, my gut churning with a mixture of fear, excitement and Alka-Seltzer.

Nevertheless, I was conscious that, underneath it all, I had enjoyed the challenge. And at the back of my mind were the beginnings of 'a thought': true, there was a hell of a long haul ahead. But, if we were very lucky we might manage to do a bit of good for a few people and it was also just possible that we might eventually be on to a winner.

Two days later came one of my first 'funny' moments on Radio 2 though like most such moments they shorten the JY life expectancy by a few years. *Aficionados* of the Prog will be familiar with the name Dr Mike Smith. He is now one of our two much loved doctors who appear on the programme regularly. On 4 July 1973, however, I had never met him. He was Head of the Family Planning Association, and I was to interview him about a proposal to issue free contraceptives. Anxious to avoid offending sensitive listeners, I decided to phrase my opening question carefully: 'Is the most widely used method of contraception still the condom, Dr Smith?' I asked.

Mike, an absolutely charming, but utterly forthright man, who calls a spade a spade and a loo a lavatory, looked at me as though I was an idiot. 'Do you by any chance mean the French letter?' he asked.

My God, I thought, day three and the sack already.

'Er, well, yes, I suppose I do', I said weakly.

'Well, if you mean French letters, why don't you say so', retorted Mike, giving me the lesson in straight talking which, clearly, he felt I needed. He proceeded to talk enthusiastically, and knowledgeably, about the merits and demerits of same.

We had only one letter of complaint, and a vast number congratulating Mike on his straightforward, unembarrassed way of explaining things. Mike had just taken his first step towards becoming a 'JY Prog' regular and I had learned that most people don't want to be 'protected' from the truth.

In the early days one of the programme's areas of interest was consumer affairs. It seemed logical, therefore, to ask the then Minister for Trade and Consumer Affairs, Sir Geoffrey Howe, if he would agree to appear.

Somewhat to my surprise on 5 July, when the programme was only three days old, he said he would. Sir Geoffrey had been accustomed to being interviewed in the more staid atmosphere of Radio 4. He had never seen someone surrounded by, and operating equipment, while at the same time conducting an interview. Clearly it fascinated him. Of course, back in July 1973, I didn't realize the little psychological edge this gave me at a time when I most desperately needed it.

Away we went and we were soon heavily into exclusion clauses, caravan-site problems, consumer rights and so on. The telephone lights flashed. The reactions poured in. Sir Geoffrey was enjoying himself. Completely involved he asked whether he could cancel a luncheon appointment and stay on to the end of the programme. 'Yes please', said I. We organized some sandwiches for him from the BBC canteen, but he was so busy broadcasting that he had no time to eat them.

So, at the end of the Prog, we were treated to the rather unusual sight of the Minister for Consumer Affairs, getting into his car, clutching three worse-for-wear BBC sandwiches to munch on his way back to the House of Commons.

Geoffrey Howe's therefore became the first ministerial bottom to sit on the 'hot seat' in Continuity 'D' at Broadcasting House.

People have often asked me what the 'hot seat' actually looks like. Well, in later years we were treated to a new one but, at that time it didn't look too hot at all. A nondescript greyish colour, it had obviously seen better days. Not to put too fine a point on it, bits of stuffing were escaping through a hole in the seat. Perhaps though, on reflection, it was in a way the smallness of the studio, the relaxed atmosphere and the 'un-stuffiness', literally in the case of the hot seat, which contributed to the success of the interviews.

I have often been asked why important people should want to talk to me and also how I've managed to get very big audiences to listen to discussions on subjects not usually regarded as 'popular'. I think one answer is that I never allow anyone to 'flannel' our audience. I totally reject gobbledegook, and I insist on replies being given in language everyone can understand.

And before the critics draw breath, let me say that does not mean asking the speaker to oversimplify, or underrate his or her audience. Plain, direct answers command more respect than any amount of clever-clever jargon or evasiveness.

A 'for instance' concerns a great friend of mine, former editor of *Punch* magazine, Bill Davis. William is a *very* bright gentleman indeed and, on 2 August 1973, he came on to the Prog to talk about financial matters. Now, as it happens, I know a little about the Stock Exchange, and Bill knew that I did. So, when I asked him the first question away he went. He addressed *me* for the best part of a minute in technical financial language.

As he paused for breath I said, on behalf of our audience, 'Bill, I haven't the faintest idea what you're on about. Could you say that again at about half the speed (he talks *very* quickly) and in language we can all understand.' I have heard Bill tell that story when I've attended one of the famous lunches at *Punch*, and say in conclusion, 'Jim was absolutely right.'

It is no good 'broadcasting to the converted', as some so-called 'serious' programmes do, and then retiring to the bar to drink large gins and tonic while telling yourself how clever you are at broadcasting to nobody. You can't communicate if there's no one listening.

Our programme formula of going live and being completely flexible can, as I have said, cause a few hairy moments. It can also, however, provide the occasional magic moment. One came my way when Sir Keith Joseph was Minister of Health. A surgeon in this country had done a heart transplant operation during which, unfortunately, the patient had died. Heart transplant operations being in their early stages at the time, Sir Keith issued a statement which suggested that perhaps surgeons might slow down on doing such operations until there was a greater likelihood of success. We were on the air when our 'flexibility factor' came into play. My chief researcher, Charles Thompson, said to me, 'Would you fancy interviewing Professor Christiaan Barnard about the Keith Joseph statement?'

'Of course,' I replied; 'where is he?'

'I haven't the faintest idea,' he said, 'but I'll find him.'

A little later he popped into the studio: 'I've tracked him down in Johannesburg, can you talk to him now?' I must point out that I have never met Professor Barnard in my life, nor had I ever previously interviewed him.

I asked him if he would comment on the Keith Joseph statement, and, when he said he would, I read it to him. I finished, and he paused for a moment. He then said, 'Can you tell me the medical qualifications of the gentleman who made this statement?' I replied that, so far as I knew, he had none. 'Then,' said Professor Barnard, 'I think he should keep his mouth shut. Good morning.' Well worth the effort, I thought.

I have several times mentioned the JY 'team' which, not unnaturally, I reckon is the best in the business. Our method of approaching an in-depth interview is that we all do our individual research, and then pool our findings. I read up every available piece of information on our subject that I can lay my hands on. This, plus my freedom to pick up points in answers and follow them through as far as I like, indeed to change the whole course of the interview if I consider it desirable, puts me in a position to cope with most situations. All this background work, which I enjoy, never fails to remind me of the well-tried boxers' maxim, 'train hard, fight easy'.

I had certainly 'trained hard' between 5 July and 14 August

because, although 5 July had been a breakthrough for us with Sir Geoffrey Howe's visit, Tuesday 14 August was to prove to be our biggest moment so far. This was the occasion of my first interview with the then Minister of Education, Mrs Margaret Thatcher. The event caused a sensation in Broadcasting House. Not only did most of BBC top management want to witness the interview; in those early days that was to be expected, but so many Press photographers turned up that they had to come in three separate 'shifts'.

Looking back one suspects that there may have been some at the very top of the BBC who were worried lest we were going too far too quickly. After all, we had only been on Radio 2 for seven weeks, and already we had been able to get interviews with both the Minister for Consumer Affairs and the Secretary of State for Education. No one said anything, you understand, and it is to the eternal credit of both Douglas and Ian that, if they *did* have any worries, they kept them to themselves. They allowed the Prog its head to develop and settle into 'doing its own thing'.

It was my first meeting with Mrs Thatcher. To say that I was nervous is putting it mildly. In terms of political interviewing, I think it would be safe to say that I was really being thrown in at the deep end. Having 'trained hard', fighters arrive in the ring mean and edgy. I didn't arrive in Con. 'D' mean, but there was no doubt that I was edgy.

Never have I been more quickly disarmed. Mrs Thatcher is one of those people in public life who have the misfortune not to 'come across' at their best on television. Having only seen her before 'on the box' I was therefore all geared up to meet the Iron Lady (a nickname not yet coined of course), but I was certainly *not* expecting to meet the lady who walked into my studio. She is much prettier than her pictures. Certainly much more feminine than I had expected. She is also the total, complete professional. In those days we sometimes did a real 'phone-in' programme. In other words we actually put the member of the public phoning in directly through to the person to whom they wanted to talk, so that they could put their question personally. This meant that, in Mrs Thatcher's case, with a large ministry to represent, she had to be prepared to deal with very wide-ranging questions, and deal with them 'off the top of her head': no advance notice of questions and so completely spontaneous answers.

I watched her deal with these questions, getting instantly on first-name terms with her callers, chatting about where they lived, involving herself as a parent, while all the time doing sums and writing replies on her notepad. It was then that I formed the opinion, and don't forget that this was when you would have got long odds against us ever having a woman Prime Minister, that I was looking at a very formidable political figure indeed. One sentence from the broadcast should, I suppose, have given us a strong clue to future events. In reply to a question about getting things done, Mrs Thatcher said, 'In politics if you want anything ask a man, but if you want anything *done* ask a woman!'

I mention Ethel de Loch for only one reason. She came on the Prog to talk about psychic acupuncture, i.e. acupuncture without using needles. Now psychic acupuncture may or may not have a great future, but it was something that she said about *my* future which particularly intrigued me. It intrigued me because it had been said twice before.

On two separate occasions, Jean Dixon, who is an American clairvoyant, and Katina Theodossiou, who is an astrologer living in London, had told me that, although I appeared to be doing quite well, I should not begin really to scale the peaks of my career until the 1980s. On 16 August 1973 on the programme, and for no reason at all since I had not asked her a question about it, Ethel de Loch said the same thing.

Ethel de Loch, Katina Theodossiou and Jean Dixon had never met, nor even talked to each other. So why should all three come up with the same timetable? Coincidence? Could be. We'll see.

The week beginning 1 October 1973 saw the Prog featured on the front cover of *Radio Times,* a much coveted honour. By the end of October not only had Geoffrey Howe and Margaret Thatcher been back to see us, but we had managed to push the frontiers of the programme out further with coverage from

Jerusalem, Beirut and Cairo of the Middle East War. Not an area of reporting which had seemed likely for me only a few short months ago on Radio 1. It is interesting, in retrospect, to see how quickly the programme was accepted as a responsible forum on which to discuss serious issues.

What also pleased me was that we were beginning to deal with subjects, such as abortion, which, as well as being serious, were also so charged with emotion that they had traditionally been thought of as extremely difficult to handle on radio.

Yet we still managed to keep in touch with the lighter side of life. On Friday 23 November, for instance, I introduced the then unknown, but now world famous, Uri Geller to a startled British public. It is generally thought that Uri was introduced to Britain on BBC Television, but this is not true. In fact, we on the programme had already stopped Britain's clocks and bent Britain's forks many hours before television tried it, as Uri makes clear in his book *My Story*. We very nearly *didn't* get Uri to bend anything at all if the truth were known. He is, as you will know if you have seen him 'on the box', an extremely good looking young man who can be absolutely charming. He is also crammed full of nervous energy and can, on occasions, be extremely temperamental. Such an occasion was on 23 November 1973 and I happened to be the lucky interviewer! It was just that Uri was fed up with bending things, and in practically his first remark to me on the air he told me so. It took me ten minutes of on-air wheeling and dealing, trying my very best to relax him before he grudgingly said, 'Oh, all right then, give me a key.' I don't know to this day what made me do what I then did, but it led to a very funny escapade, for somebody else!

Although I had my door keys in my pocket I turned to my chief researcher, Charles Thompson, and said: 'I haven't got my keys on me, Charles. Could you lend Uri one of yours?' Charles, perhaps not fully believing the stories about Uri anyway, obligingly produced what later turned out to be the key to the front door of his flat. Uri rubbed it gently with a finger and the key gradually began to bend. He then put it down on the desk in front of us and said, 'There's now no need for me to touch it any more, it will just continue to bend.' Sure enough, it did. And what's more it kept right on doing so until it had bent to an angle of about thirty degrees.

It was only the next morning when Charles came in to work that I heard how the story had ended. The day's work done, Charles went home to his first-floor flat in Chelsea. It was then that he made the discovery that his front door key and his front door lock no longer had anything even remotely in common. The lock simply refused to allow the key to enter. All, however, was not lost. Charles's flat had a balcony. It also had french windows which were open. And as though all that were not enough there was a bus stop immediately opposite, just made to order. Charles being a product of Millfield School was fairly athletic. Up the bus stop sign he went as to the manner born. He had one hand and foot on the sign and one hand and foot on his balcony railings when it happened. "Ello 'ello 'ello,' said the voice from below, 'what's all this then sir?' Constable Plod of the Chelsea nick had struck. As I said just now, at this time Uri Geller was completely unknown in Britain. You can easily imagine therefore the quaint little scene. Charles attempting to explain things to the policeman, 'Well, it's like this officer, I work on the "JY Prog", and this morning this geezer bent my front door key by gently rubbing it with his fingers.' No chance. Charles's rescue from the clutches of the Law finally came when his wife arrived at the flat with her 'Un-Uri'd' front door key.

I wasn't too popular for a couple of days.

Looking back, the change of direction taken by the Prog over the first eight months seemed remarkable. We had speedily won a huge audience for discussions on important and often complex topics. We could still, however, produce the occasional odd item.

In 1974, for instance, I informed a world, no doubt eager for such knowledge, that left-over egg yolks are very popular with cats. I interviewed the World Champion Organ Playing Marathon Record Holder (he played for fifty-three hours and two minutes in case you're interested!) while at the same time announcing that I should shortly be dealing with the results of the forthcoming General Election in a 'Jimmy Young Election

Special'. In later years the 'Jimmy Young Election Special' programmes became something of a tradition. However, back in
1974, it was a sensation for Radio 2 to be attempting anything
of this kind. There were a few furrowed brows and sweaty
palms but 'Auntie', and full marks to her again for giving the
Prog its head, held her breath and the experiment went on.

They gave me tried and trusted BBC political expert, Brian
Curtois, to see I didn't actually fall over the furniture, but apart
from that, we stuck to our usual basic format.

Came the day and we moved into the much bigger Studio
4A, on the fourth floor of Broadcasting House. Studio 4A has
a quite large semi-circular table. Rising from the centre of the
table is a cluster of microphones, making it possible for me to
talk to six people at any one sitting. Added to that there were
television screens for feeding in election results, desks for secretaries, researchers, and the occasional newsreader, and I
speedily saw that we could never have done the programme
from our small, homely Continuity 'D'.

The 'JY Programme' is always a team effort, of course, but
never more so than on occasions like these. Everybody's homework is important. Everybody has a vital job to do. The producer keeps a watchful eye overall. Researchers move
smoothly, but quickly, with news of arriving guests, and details of interviews coming up on lines or telephones. And
always instantly to hand is all the information on candidates,
constituencies, margins and swings, which is necessary to enable Brian and myself to broadcast. It's exciting, stimulating,
and incredibly busy. It is also, when properly organized,
usually calm. Almost as though everyone is deliberately in
third gear rather than panic overdrive.

The programme producer has another, not usually publi-
cized, job at times like these. Senior management, on important occasions, sometimes organize small parties. After drinks
and snacks, and as the night wears on, they often tour the
building and pop into studios for a visit. Those are the times
when, in the thick of things, one sometimes looks up to see
perhaps a dozen faces peering through the studio window.
You understand, quite suddenly, how the pandas in the zoo
feel. You also see the programme staff getting increasingly

irritated as they find themselves unable to move. And that is where the producer comes in. He has to persuade the beautiful people, tactfully of course, to get the hell out of it, without getting us all the sack. It's sometimes not easy I can tell you.

Anyway, while I was learning how exciting such events could be, I was also making another discovery. Politicians and trade union leaders are not necessarily devoid of a sense of humour. As when Hughie Scanlon dropped in to talk to me on an Election Special. I asked him if he would, as we say in the trade, 'give a bit for level'. That is, I was asking him to say a few words which would not be broadcast, but which would enable the studio manager to get a balanced level on his voice. On the first try he was a little 'off mike'. The studio manager put down the talk back key on his side of the soundproof glass. 'Could you move a little to the left Mr Scanlon?' he said.

'Anytime, my boy,' boomed Hughie, 'anytime.'

In 1974 we established the basic mix of the programme. Our watchword was 'variety': Sir Michael Havers, Shadow Solicitor General, whose son Nigel was working on the programme at the time; Minister of Sport Denis Howell on soccer violence; John Methven, then Director of Fair Trading; Ulster; the Flixborough disaster; dried cat food; E.E.C. mountains; the Cyprus crisis; Reg Freeson, Minister of Housing; the Nixon resignation; the tragedy of Maria Colwell; Lord Longford; and then, on 9 September, the Chancellor of the Exchequer, Denis Healey.

It was about this time that controversy was raging over my calling well-known people by their Christian names. 'How dare he', and all that stuff. It had come about in the most innocent way. When we began interviewing famous people I said to my producer, 'Would you ask them what they would like me to call them, please?' This he did and, whether it is because of the small, intimate nature of the studio, or because of the informal atmosphere in which we operate I do not know but, almost without exception they said, 'Oh, Christian names, please.' So Geoffrey Howe became Geoffrey, Margaret Thatcher became Margaret, and so on. Very few it seemed liked to use formal titles, but of course, if they did, then that was how I addressed them.

22

I hadn't the faintest idea how I would get on with Denis Healey who can appear, and indeed *is* a formidable figure. He sorted it out as soon as we were introduced. He knew something which I didn't, and it was nothing to do with his budgets either. His opening line was, 'I'll bet you didn't know your mother used to play the piano for my mother-in-law to sing.' By an odd coincidence his mother-in-law, Mrs Rose Edmunds, sang in the same church choir in the Forest of Dean in Gloucestershire as did my mother, who also played the piano. Indeed, Mrs Edmunds, who sang so beautifully that she was known as 'The Nightingale of the Forest', spoke of my dear old mum as 'a very talented pianist, and a delightful lady'. Denis had obviously done *his* homework and, after a start like that, it just *had* to be Denis, didn't it?

This was the broadcast when Denis announced, to my considerable surprise, that inflation was running at something like eight and a half per cent. I didn't actually say 'silly Billy' but I did voice the opinion that it was, perhaps, running at a rate which was, shall we be discreet and say, somewhat higher.

One of the nice things about Denis is that he's such a *big* man. The voice, the eyebrows, the extrovert personality, the sense of humour and the laugh. Even when he's in his 'squeezing the pips' mood of rhetoric it's almost impossible to dislike him. At any rate I found it so. At one stage I asked him a particularly probing question which just *could* have been taken personally. As the next record was playing, I said, 'Nothing personal intended, Denis.'

Quick as a flash, and still smiling he answered, 'If I thought there had been I'd have come round there and knocked your head off.' You have to warm to a leading politician who has a sense of humour like that. At least, I *think* he was joking.

Denis was followed a couple of days later by the Right Hon. Robert Carr, Shadow Chancellor, and a few days after that by the Liberal Spokesman on the economy at that time, John Pardoe. All these appearances by leading figures were, as you can well imagine, of the greatest interest to our friends in the Press. Of the Chancellor's appearance, *The Sun* of 10 September 1974 headlined, 'Oft we jolly well go on the DH Prog' and said, of Denis, 'He surprisingly chose Jimmy's Radio 2 show to make his first statement on his weekend secret meeting with world finance ministers.' Of Shadow Chancellor Robert Carr's appearance, Shaun Usher in the *Daily Mail* on 12 September said: 'Jimmy Young pounced on the famous Tory Manifesto leak. One gathered JY felt that Carr's non-subliminal election-eering was heavy going, since he peppered it with several record breaks, more than he considered needful for Healey. With Mr Carr,' said Shaun, 'it's a clear case of don't call us, we'll call you.'

Incidentally, any member of the lay public reading this may have wondered why, when you have seen the Chancellor of the Exchequer doing his thing, you are also required to see the Shadow Chancellor, the Liberal Spokesman and so on. It's all down to a little thing which political and current affairs pro-grammes refer to as 'balance'. Balance is the theory that all decent chaps must have a fair crack of the whip, and that all decent current affairs chaps must see that they do. From time to time your programme statistics are sent for by the powers that be, and the numbers of M.P.s of different persuasions whom you have interviewed must balance just about evenly. Most of the time it works out very well, but the rules, like any others, are capable of being bent if the person concerned has a will so to do. Like the time when a lady current affairs person of far left persuasion was mounting a three-handed interview programme and said to me, 'I've got a brilliant Labour speaker, a wishy washy Liberal, now all I want is a burke of a Con-servative and I've got a balanced programme.' Only she didn't say burke. Not of course that one would ever admit that there are any really thick M.P.s, it's just that some are not quite as brilliant as others.

We had now been on the air just over a year and interest in the Prog kept growing. So did our listening figures, by leaps and bounds. We were even beginning to make the 'heavy papers'. Highly respected writer, Gillian Reynolds, said in the *Guardian*, 'Educated consumers may laugh, sophisticated BBC planners may shudder, but I would bet a pound to a privet hedge that it's Jim's show the commercial boys will be listening to and learning from.'

3- People on the Prog

It wasn't all politics though. We got a request for help from a compulsive gambler. His name wasn't John but that, for the purpose of the programme, was what we called him. He had lost three businesses and £60,000 through gambling and just wasn't able to give it up. However, he was trying, and wanted to come on the programme to tell people what a really serious problem gambling could become. He also thought that if he could have a target to aim at, in our case to come back in a year and tell us how he was getting on, he just might be able to break the habit. I don't know where he is now of course, but at least he came back to us in 1975 and again in 1976 and said he had managed to last that long. The only trouble was, he said, he had been beaten up by some of the bookies with whom he used to gamble. Obviously the gambler's success was his bookie's loss!

I'd often heard of a 'no-win situation'. John seemed to have found it.

As had a Senior Citizen who wrote to us with a very personal problem indeed, which managed to be both funny and extremely poignant at the same time. He had been fortunate enough to have enjoyed a long and happy marriage. Unfortunately his wife had very suddenly died. In his letter he sounded both lonely and depressed. He was also obviously a fit and healthy gentleman, who missed every comfort formerly provided by his late spouse. He had tried, and failed, to find himself another partner, and therefore decided that, as a temporary solution to his physical problem, he would, so to speak, try a different approach. Accordingly, he purchased, by mail order, one of those inflatable rubber dolls, of which of course, the more sheltered of our readers will not have heard. In due course nature provided both the need and the moment. Eagerly, our correspondent inflated his surrogate lover. He sought to make her closer, nay intimate, acquaintance. Unfortunately all that happened was a rush of air from one of her ruptured seams and she shrank to the size of a small wizened monkey. Feeling, to say the least, frustrated by the way he had been let down by his mail order firm, he returned her to them, with an indignant letter. They sent him a new one. Three days later exactly the same thing happened.

With an even stiffer letter he returned doll number two and, increasingly frustrated and impatient, he awaited the arrival of a brand new, super-sealed, non-leaky lover. What he actually got was doll number two returned, plus a cycle tube repair kit. He wrote to us, most aggrieved, to complain about manufacturing standards. I'm afraid though that not even our experts could do much on the air about that one.

There are certain subjects which we know in advance are bound to bring in an immediate flood of telephone calls, shortly to be followed by an avalanche of letters. Euthanasia is one of them.

Firm attitudes are taken by the pros and antis and one is never really likely to change them. Not, of course, that we try on the programme. We merely report the public's reaction.

George Mair is a surgeon. He is a Scotsman with a healthy, robust approach to life, a ready laugh and a great sense of humour. He's a really terrific guy. He is also the man who wrote a book called *Confessions of a Surgeon*. He told on the programme of how in 1939 he was treating a woman in her forties who was in a hopeless condition. She was riddled with cancer and in great, almost unendurable, pain. One day, during a ward round, she asked him, 'Will you help me out? I've had a hairdo, I've said goodbye to all the people I love. Will you bring my favourite record of Beethoven's Ninth and give me a jab while the record is playing?' Those are George's exact words as he spoke them on the programme. He then went on, 'She held my hand, and when she asked I gave her the jab. A little while later when she was about to fall asleep, and at that stage I do mean fall asleep, she looked at me with real gratitude and with real love.'

There was a massive reaction to the interview, polarized into two bodies of opinion: those who speak of blessed relief, and those who speak of the sin of it all, and the Lord's will being done. As in all other subjects with which we deal I regard it as my job to present as many views on the topic as we can to stimulate thoughts, reaction and discussion, but not to force my own opinion on people. Which does not, of course, mean that on euthanasia, as on many other matters, I do not have my own views.

I must record however, that the vast majority of the phoned-in public reaction to the George Mair interview was in favour of George's pro-euthanasia viewpoint.

I rather wondered whether George might get arrested. He didn't.

One of the great things about my post-1973 job is that I have met some legendary figures. One may have varying views about the merits or otherwise of American politicians in general, and the Kennedy family in particular. However, the Kennedys are, and because of the history books, are always going to be, fascinating.

I was just about to meet the matriarch. My mother was a small lady, but standing next to Rose Kennedy she would have been much the bigger of the two. Into my studio walked the tiniest, oh so frail creature. So tiny that, because the guest seat on the other side of the studio from me is rather high, we replaced it with a much lower chair. Even so some extremely tactful assistance was necessary to see that she got on to it safely. What a formidable lady, though. Tough. No nonsense. Replies to questions smiling, but aggressive. Yet during the whole of the interview the one thing that really fascinated me was the fact that, out of the womb of the tiny lady sitting opposite me had come all those strapping men of the Kennedy clan. By the time the interview was over, there was no doubt in my mind who had the last word in the Kennedy family.

As far as the Prog was concerned, I fear the cries of 'Happy New Year' 1975 and the afterglow of the seasonal festivities were not to last very long. As early into the New Year as 2 January, battling Barbara Castle was on the programme confronting the doctors, and in particular Dr Brian Lewis whom *The Sun* newspaper described as the 'Militant Doctors' Leader'. Well, to be absolutely honest she didn't actually confront the good doctor since, due to an elaborate game of musical chairs we had invented, they never met.

Dr Lewis spoke first on the programme while Mrs Castle listened in a separate room. He was then shunted into an empty studio and the curtains drawn so that he couldn't see Mrs Castle while she was talking to me. Why all the fuss? I haven't the faintest idea. Anyway, we ended up with massive Press coverage and, as to the reasons for the 'non-meeting' you can take your pick out of three, together with the quotes:

Dr Brian 'Consultants are fed up to the teeth' Lewis, who said: 'I understood she didn't want us to go on together.'

Mrs Barbara 'Doctors hold a pistol at my head' Castle, who said: 'I was never asked to appear with Dr Lewis.'

Or your traditional and ubiquitous BBC spokesman who said: 'There was no reason why they should meet.'

Anyway it all added to the mystery and provided the Press with good copy, but it is the only interview I have ever had to conduct under such unusual circumstances.

Wednesday 19 February 1975 saw me opening an interview with the words, 'It's just a week since the political world was shaken up with the news that a woman is to lead one of Britain's major political parties. Mrs Margaret Thatcher emerged triumphant from the second ballot for the leadership of the Conservative Party after two weeks of battling with the then leader Mr Heath, and of course other prominent elder statesmen.'

I asked Mrs Thatcher what was her reaction to the previous week's happening. She said, 'I've had so much to do that I haven't really come to the surface. One still hasn't really realized that the Leader of the Opposition is me.' I asked whether she thought the contest for the leadership would have damaged the image of the Party. Mrs Thatcher replied, 'I don't think it's damaged the image of the Party, but I do of course feel very sorry for Mr Heath. Obviously one would be for a person you've worked with for quite a time.' I then asked her whether she had seen the newspaper article which, that morning, had described the overnight announcement of her Shadow Cabinet as 'The night of the long hat pin'. 'I hadn't seen that', she said; 'oh, my goodness.' It's an odd thing that this dedicated strong-minded politician has still retained an almost school-girlish little corner in her nature which will sometimes allow her to pop out a line like, 'Oh, my goodness.' Almost an 'Oh, golly gosh.'

We are often reminded by political writers that a political leader must be a good butcher. This, they say, is absolutely essential. But you can be a good butcher without getting blood all over the shop, as Mrs Thatcher was about to demonstrate. I had, on the previous day, interviewed Peter Walker on the programme. Peter had been dropped from the Shadow Cabinet. I decided to ask her about it. 'What about the people who are *not* going to play a part in the Shadow Cabinet, people like Geoffrey Rippon, Robert Carr and Peter Walker?' I asked.

Said Margaret, smoothly, 'Well, after all, you need a lot of talent on your backbenches in Parliament too. It's not always just those who are on the frontbenches. I think it adds greatly to the backbenches to have people on them who've had some experience of what it's like to be in office. Peter will be a great asset on the backbenches and so will Geoffrey Rippon and some of the others.'

Later in the interview I actually asked Margaret whether she was a good butcher. She said, 'I don't know whether I'm a good one. I'm a reluctant one, but I recognize it is one of the tests of leadership.'

It is always interesting to look back on what politicians have said prior to their achieving power, and then to measure it against their sayings and doings when in power.

In that respect one has to admit that Margaret Thatcher is

most certainly consistent. Back in February 1975 I asked her, in this same interview: 'What, in your opinion, is the root cause of Britain's problems?'

Said Mrs Thatcher, 'We won't face inflation, and won't face the fact that, ultimately, you've *got* to pay your way.'

'Which begs the next question', said I; 'suppose you were put into No. 10 tomorrow, at a stroke so to speak, what would you do?'

'Tackle inflation sternly', said Mrs Thatcher; 'and you can't do that without taking unpleasant measures.'

As I write this in 1982 any 'JY Prog' listeners unhappy with the Conservative Government's policies must admit that they had clear enough warning!

Life, however, was not just about interviewing leading politicians. Indeed, we included at that time a few items which, in this day and age, we might think to be a little too light for us.

Thus it came about that, two days after interviewing the brand new Leader of the Conservative Party, I was talking to Mr Charles Roberts. You may not immediately recognize the name and if you don't, I, for one, wouldn't be surprised. Just the same, Charles had his own claim to fame. He professed to have grown the world's largest tomato, and he brought it into the studio to show us. Certainly it was enormous, but it wasn't the tomato itself, so much as the way he alleged he had grown it, that intrigued us. You see, Charles claimed to have discovered that his tomato plants thrived by listening to the 'JY Prog'. No one else's voice seemed to have any effect on them at all, but once JY got into his stride the little beauties simply blossomed. 'What is more,' said Charles, 'when you aren't on the radio at the weekend they pine for you so much that I find their growth suffers.'

'How do you cope with that?' I asked.

'Oh,' said Charles, 'I record the programmes that you do from Monday to Friday. I've fixed them all up with their own individual headphones, and I play the recorded programmes back to them on Saturdays and Sundays. It works a treat.' Sure enough, he produced a picture from the local newspaper showing all his tomatoes sitting there with their headphones on, looking for all the world like row upon row of lovely chubby pink disc jockeys. As I said in the *Sunday Mirror*: 'Just fancy. I've been talking to a load of sensitive adolescent tomatoes for months and I never knew.' I think old Charlie was pulling my leg really, but it made a nice little fun story just the same.

Back in July 1973 I had interviewed the new Minister for Consumer Affairs, and now, in March 1975 I was due to meet another one. This one, however, was of a different party and a different sex. It was Mrs Shirley Williams; Shirley, of the unkempt hair and clothes, about whom everybody always has a nice word to say. I could see why when I met her. She was delightful. I put it to her that she had often been put forward as the country's first potential woman Prime Minister, so how did she feel about Mrs Thatcher's success in the Conservative Party leadership election? Did she think she would be pipped at the post? Said Shirley, 'I think it's high time we forgot about whether people are men or women and judge them according to what they can contribute to the country. I'll be quite frank about it, I think Mrs Thatcher's a very capable woman and a very intelligent one. I'm pleased to see that people have to take her seriously.' Well said. But hold on, were there any reservations? Yes, there was one. 'So, I'm pleased when she does well as a woman, and not so pleased when she does well as a Conservative!' That's more like it.

So much for the politician. But did you know that our Shirley was also a not inconsiderable actress? You didn't? Nor did I. But then I learn something new on the Prog almost every day.

In the mid-1940s it so happened that Shirley was in the United States when film critics were asked to put forward the name of someone who might be suitable to star in a film which was being put together. It was about a girl who owns a horse which is on the way to the knackers' yard, and can only be saved by winning a very famous race. The girl had to be English, she had to be about twelve, she had to be able to ride. (If you're over forty, is the name of the film coming back to you yet?) The short-list totalled seven, including Shirley Williams.

Also on the short-list however was Elizabeth Taylor, and she it was who went on to star in *National Velvet*. Nonetheless as

Shirley said to me, 'I suppose I did have my moment of glory.

Shirley also toured as Cordelia in *King Lear*, living, as she said, from one hamburger stand to the next, all over the United States of America.

I asked her, 'I know you didn't take up acting professionally, but have you found your interest in acting an asset in politics?' Said Shirley, 'It's no good denying that there's some link between the two. We've got some first class actors in the House of Commons.' I reckon we'd all go along with that.

Thursday 5 June 1975 was an important date of course, that being the date of the Common Market Referendum. We decided that, since the programme's policy was one of maximum audience involvement, and since this was to be such an historically important decision, we would involve our audience to the fullest possible extent.

Accordingly, I trailed the fact that, if our listeners would like to send in the questions which they most wanted to be asked, we would mount a special programme and do the best we could to get them answered.

We were up to our eyeballs in letters before you could say 'Yes/No'. Far from mounting one 'Common Market Referendum Special' programme, as had been our intention, the interest shown by our listeners was so great that we had to mount three. On 6 May 1975 I interviewed anti-Marketeer Tony Benn in the studio and pro-Marketeer George Thomson on the line from Brussels. On 13 May, anti-Marketeer Hugh Scanlon crossed swords with pro-Marketeer Sir Frederick Catherwood, and on 22 May, it was the turn of anti-Marketeer Mrs Mary Blakey, President of the British Housewives' League and pro-Marketeer Sir Henry Plumb, President of the National Farmers Union. We on the programme did not, of course, take sides in the matter, nor did we set out to influence decisions. But at the end of the three programmes we felt that we had achieved what has always been the object of our particular exercise; we had got the pros and cons thoroughly aired by people in authority, talking the kind of language which people at all levels could understand. The phone-in reaction was enormous. The switchboard was jammed. So much for the knockers who, less than two years before, had been confidently predicting that the 'Great British Public' would not be in the least interested in what was going on in the world around them!

The programme has also enjoyed considerable success over the years in helping people in trouble. As I write this we have just mounted a very successful week-long campaign to help the Manpower Services Commission. We were asked if we would try to find employers who would be willing to take on an extra employee under the Youth Opportunities Scheme. And, in just five days, we turned up 2,000 employers who declared that they would be willing to do so. It was an immensely rewarding experience for us on the programme and I think even the Manpower Services Commission were surprised by the success of our campaign.

Back in 1975, however, the campaign was all about literacy. The BBC was planning to run a 'Literacy Referal Programme' and I had been asked if I would do a 'trial run' by explaining on my programme what this was all about. It was felt that even people who actually needed a literacy programme might be rather reluctant to come forward and take part, and that an explanation on the 'JY Prog' would help. A switchboard was made available, manned by eight people who, it was certain, would be more than enough to deal with any enquiries. Clearly, whoever had done the planning had underestimated 'the Prog' because as soon as I mentioned the proposed scheme, 600 telephone calls immediately jammed the switchboard, and senior administrators and their secretaries, plus six members of the team working on the series, had to be rushed over in taxis to cope. Interestingly enough, of the 600 calls, almost 350 came from people who could neither read nor write, over 100 were from people ringing on behalf of relatives or friends, and 130 were from people who wanted to help teach. I know do-gooders can be a bit of a pain sometimes, but at times like these, and more recently with the Youth Opportunities Scheme, using the media to assist people who really need help can be a very warm and satisfying experience.

In October 1975 I interviewed Robin Day, who was of course

more used to asking the questions himself. We were talking about Robin's book called, *Day by Day: a dose of my own hemlock.*

It was interesting to compare our techniques, since in the early stages they are very similar: we both do a massive amount of homework, and aim to be thoroughly briefed by the time of the broadcast. When we come to the interview, though, we operate differently. Robin, of course, is famous for the hunched shoulders, the 'cruel glasses', the inquisitorial stare and the rough edge to the voice. I, by contrast, operate in a, seemingly, much less abrasive way. I prefer what journalist Gillian Reynolds once referred to as 'the polite but persistent probing of Mr Jimmy Young'. Both styles seem effective since we both appear to be able to extract headline-making quotes from famous people. A line in Robin's book intrigued me, however, because in it he admits that, 'An interview may look tough and sound searching, but in reality may have only scraped the surface.' Quite so. There is a story told about Robin which I like. It is said that he was talking one day to a friend of his, a very senior and distinguished BBC person. Said Robin, 'Why is it that people think you're such a nice guy when you're actually a shit, whereas everybody thinks I'm a shit when I'm really a *very* nice guy.' He is too.

I was in the news in December 1975 and January 1976 for two entirely different reasons. To begin with, I joined the National Union of Journalists, and a few days later they called the first journalists' strike at the BBC. For the first time in a twenty-six year career, which had included the membership of three trade unions, I found myself on strike. The front page headlines did nothing to ease the situation. Some, if looked at casually, seemed to suggest the whole thing was my idea!

Then, in Bedford Crown Court, a witness claimed he was sure he had spotted an accused man at the time he said he had because he had heard a time check on the 'JY Prog'.

Said defending barrister, Mr Robert Marshall-Andrews, 'Jimmy Young is extremely reliable at giving out the time.'

Said the Judge, 'Who is Jimmy Young?'

Said Mr Martin Bowley, prosecuting, 'I think you will hit the headlines.'

Said the *Daily Mirror*, 'Roars of laughter in court.'

On 5 April 1976 an era in British political history ended. Harold Wilson, who had been Leader of the Labour Party since 1963 and Prime Minister on two separate occasions, stepped down, and Jim Callaghan was duly appointed Prime Minister by the Queen. One of the people closest to Harold Wilson during all those years in high office was his secretary, Marcia Williams or, as she had now become, Lady Falkender. She had never been noted for giving many interviews but the next day, 6 April, we decided to ask whether she would come in to the studio and talk to me about the historic happenings of the previous day. She said she would be pleased to.

It was a full two years later, incidentally, that I learned from a famous lady journalist that this interview caused particular heartsearching at the morning meeting of one well-known newspaper. In stormed the editor. 'What the hell's wrong with all of you?' he cried. 'We've been trying for a bloody year to get an interview with Marcia Williams and, immediately following Wilson's resignation, up she pops on the bloody "Jimmy Young Programme".' Ah well, you can't please 'em all.

Anyway, back to the interview of 6 April 1976. As she entered the studio I said, 'Good morning, Lady Falkender.'

'Good morning, Jimmy,' she replied, 'but I'm happier to be called Marcia in fact, so I do hope you'll call me that.' We had another Christian name to add to our list!

Marcia, rather like Mrs Thatcher at least in one respect, is a lady who 'comes across' much better when you're actually with her than she does when you are watching her on the box. It's true to say that on television she does give the impression of suffering a touch of the Esther Rantzen's but, when you are with her, the teeth are nowhere near as prominent. She is an attractive, warm, highly intelligent, and most charming person. I asked her opinion of Mr Wilson. 'He is', she said, 'an absolutely marvellous man to work with. Calm, quiet, understanding, and experienced. He has sound judgement, a great brain, great ability. You feel you can depend on him. He brought peace to the Labour Party and, I think, in the last two years he has brought peace to the country.' I asked her how good she was at predicting the outcome of general elections. 'Not too good', she said; 'in 1966 I thought we might lose, so I ordered up the removal vans, packed everything up, and we emerged with an enormous majority. In 1970 I thought, well, I was wrong last time so perhaps I'll be right this time, maybe we'll win. We lost.' She also had very strong views on the actual changeover of tenancy at No. 10 Downing Street, after an election. She thought the present scramble to get the defeated gladiator out and the new incumbent installed, to say the least, terribly undignified. She said, 'I think when there is a changeover of two different political parties there ought to be a new arrangement where the outgoing Prime Minister could have some time with the incoming Prime Minister to tell him (her?) just what sort of problems he's going to be faced with. Certainly I would like to see the present system changed.'

Perhaps here I could do Lady Falkender a small service by airing a grievance she had. In her book, *Inside Number 10*, she had written that she was critical of the Civil Service. I asked her about it. She answered, 'Yes, I wrote that I was critical of the Civil Service, and I still have great criticism of them. But no one ever pointed out the bit in my book where I say that I think we have probably one of the best Civil Services in the world.' She went on, 'I've never been given credit for saying that, so I'm getting it on the record now.' I asked her about her relationship with the Press. She was very forthright. She said, 'They've been very unkind. They've used me as a sort of punch bag. If they wanted to have a go at Mr Wilson and didn't quite want to do it on that occasion they had a go at me instead. I was a sitting target because I was a woman who had got to the top, and therefore I caught the eye more than a man would have done in the same position. They've been unkind, and it has hurt.'

We ended on the black humour subject of the 'working funeral'. I mentioned the long, and often odd, hours which politicians work. Working lunches, working breakfasts, 'But,' said I, 'at one point in your book you even refer to "working funerals".'

'Ah,' said Marcia, 'the working funeral. That's a fairly new development, and I agree that it's a very unfortunate phrase. But you see, on many occasions, statesmen dying overseas provide an opportunity for others from all over the world to gather together and sneak in a long discussion at a working funeral.'

The mind boggles at the thought of a Head of State using this new development to, if you'll pardon the expression, kill two birds with one stone. First arrange the untimely demise of an overseas Head of State whom you particularly dislike. Then arrange to attend his funeral for important discussions and you could, I suppose, be said to be combining business with pleasure.

Someone holding different political views whom I was look-ing forward to interviewing on the programme was Edward Heath. Ted talks fluently on almost any subject. Inflation, unemployment, trade unions, referenda, the Labour Party, the Liberal Party, and his view of Sir Keith Joseph's Centre for Policy Studies; 'I don't think it has made any positive contri-bution to the thinking in the Party, in fact I think it's given our opponents an opportunity for trying to divide us.' How-ever, directly I asked the question that I knew all my listeners would be wanting me to ask, Ted displayed, as I had known he would, footwork of the quality which would have made Muhammad Ali in his prime look like an amateur. The ques-tion, of course, was, 'I'm sure life as a backbencher is very nice, but wouldn't you get more done if you joined Mrs Thatcher in the Shadow Cabinet?' Or, as two of our phone-in listeners, a Mrs Moore of Battle and Mr Robert Boyd-Harwell put it, 'When are you going to stop sulking and start backing Mrs Thatcher?' We never did get an answer. But then, I re-flected, nor had any other interviewer.

I am often asked, 'Who is the most interesting person you have interviewed?' That I find an impossible question to an-swer. Not for fear of upsetting people who may imagine them-selves to be more interesting than they actually are, but because I find people fascinating in so many different ways. It's rather akin to asking someone who has been singing professionally for a quarter of a century to name his favourite song. You will probably discover he has got a dozen. No, a much easier question to answer is, 'Who is the, shall we say, most unusual person you have ever interviewed?' Quite high on that list would have to be Sir Keith Joseph. Keith, the red flag's red rag, is, I am convinced, a much misunderstood man. Having interviewed him many times I am in no doubt that he is a very good, very kind man. He is much given, as you will know, to living within one's means, good housekeeping, hard work, industry and enterprise, and to the strong and capable supplying financial safety nets to support the weak and not so capable. The only trouble is, it never quite comes out like that. When Keith says it, it tends to sound like cold showers and self-flagellation. Add to this the fact that when in full verbal flow his eyes stare and a vein throbs in his temple and you have the reason for his House of Commons affectionate nickname, The Mad Monk. He can also on occasions be slightly, and lovably, eccentric. On one occasion his eccentricity surfaced in the foyer of Broadcasting House. My producer, Harry Walters, had, as is his custom, met him at the front door. He escorted Sir Keith across the reception area to the steps leading up to my first-floor studio. They commenced to climb. Harry was leading the way, chatting as he went until, nearing the top of the stairs, he realized he was getting no answers to his conversation. He also had the odd feeling that he was alone. He stopped and looked back. Sir Keith had come to a halt. His right foot was on the third step from the bottom. His left foot was poised over the fourth step, but had made no contact with the ground. It was poised in mid-air. Our distinguished guest was bent over double, contemplating his left shoe with intense concentration. Convinced that the great man had suffered a seizure of some kind and was unable to move Harry rushed back down the stairs. 'Are you all right Sir Keith?' he cried.

'Yes, I'm fine Harry,' said Sir Keith, never moving his gaze away from his left shoe, 'I've just had a thought.'

4-The Prog at the Palace

You will have gathered by now that the programme needs, about as much as a hole in the head, a man who sits in a canvas chair with 'producer' stencilled on the back, clicking a stopwatch, and shouting 'Cue Jim' from time to time. No, our senior producer has to be what we are fortunate to have; a combination of managing director, diplomat at home and abroad, plus politician supreme, both outside and inside Broadcasting House – with the additional ability, when defending the programme, to shoot accurately from the hip. As more than one senior executive has discovered with pained surprise. However, possibly the description of my producer, Harry Walters which I like best, came to me one day, direct from the Prime Minister. 'Tell me, Jimmy,' said Mrs Thatcher, 'who is that absolutely charming, grey-haired, distinguished-looking gentleman who meets me at the front door of Broadcasting House when I come to see you?'

For the programme the high spot of 1976 came with our first visit to Buckingham Palace. We had asked His Royal Highness Prince Philip, The Duke of Edinburgh, if he would grant an interview in connection with the Queen's Award to Industry. To the delight of all of us working on the programme he agreed, provided we were able to go to Buckingham Palace to pre-record it. Came the day and Harry and I, plus our usual crack engineering team, piled into my car and set off for the

Palace. We rolled up to the front gate. The friendly copper on duty said, 'Hello Jim, park your car in the usual place, over there against the wall.' He made it sound as though I was in the habit of dropping into Buck House for tea and cakes every afternoon of the week. In fact, of course, I'd never in my life been there before. Ahead of us was an open door with a red carpet. Not laid especially for me, I hasten to add. We agreed that I would drop Harry, the engineers, and all the recording gear at the door, and that they would wait for me there while I parked the car. This we did. Buckingham Palace, close up, is pretty overpowering. Its sheer size for one thing, and the awareness of the hundreds of years of pomp and ceremony associated with it get to you, whoever you are. Especially on your first visit.

Having parked my car, I trudged across the vast forecourt towards the entrance. I was watched with idle curiosity by the fifty or so people who, at any given time, stand with their faces pressed against the outside railings, waiting for something to happen. Sure enough, something *did* happen. A voice cried out. It rang around the whole of the Palace. And even as I heard it, I realized that it was not just *one* voice, but fifty voices, orchestrated as one. Loud enough to be heard as far away as Victoria Station the voice asked, 'What's the recipe today, Jim?' It was a moment that could have made me wish the ground would open and swallow me up, but in fact it was just what the doctor ordered. I doubled up with laughter. So did the crowd standing outside the railings. In an instant my nerves disappeared.

We went into the Palace, were shown up to one of the drawing-rooms, and engineer Alan Wilson began to set up his recording equipment. I had never before met The Duke of Edinburgh and I was very much looking forward to doing so. However, I was slightly worried about this particular interview. We had been asked to supply a list of my questions in advance, and this we had done. My worry was that this might prevent me getting the fresh, unrehearsed answers essential for a good interview. It might also prevent me from putting what are known in the trade as 'follow up supplementaries'.

A door opened and Prince Philip entered, looking youthful,

tanned and very fit. He shook hands with all of us, sat down on a sofa, beckoned to me to sit next to him, and immediately struck up a conversation. He has tremendous charm, and the wonderful gift of being able to make you feel instantly at ease. Indeed, within a couple of minutes we all felt as though we really *did* pop in to Buckingham Palace on a regular basis for tea and cucumber sandwiches. Eventually we were ready to begin.

The Duke of Edinburgh checked that my list of questions was balanced comfortably on his knee. I fired Question One. He had done his homework and out came the answer. On to Question Two. During the course of the answer Prince Philip said something that intrigued me. Dare I depart from the list and ask a supplementary? I wondered. I dared. Back came the answer, fluent and fresh, and that led to another supplementary. Was I doing the right thing though? I asked myself. I got my answer as the Duke removed the list of questions from his knee and put them on the sofa beside him. He never glanced at them again throughout the rest of the interview. This had already been a very special day for me, but when we had finished Prince Philip made it even more special by commending me on the way I had conducted the interview. He said, 'You know, the thing I like about your interviewing technique is that you actually listen to the answers.'

'Oh,' said I, 'I thought you were supposed to.'

'You are,' said The Duke, 'but most people don't.'

As we drove out of the gate I wondered whether I would ever go to Buckingham Palace again. I never dreamed for a moment that my next visit would be in December 1979, and would provide the opening chapter for this book.

A bizarre thing happened to me in September 1976. It is my custom to sleep in the nude. My routine in the morning is to rise at about 6.45, make the tea, collect all the papers and then take the tea and newspapers to bed to start work. By 8 o'clock I have read them all, made the necessary notes, and am ready to talk to my chief researcher who calls me on the telephone from Broadcasting House. We compare notes and set up the basics of the morning programme. While doing all this I find it comfortable to work lying either on, or in, the bed with no clothes on. One morning in September 1976 I was working away when the door bell rang. Blow it, I thought, or words to that effect, it must be the postman with a parcel which is too big to go through the letter box. I put on a dressing-gown and went to the door. I opened it. Standing outside was a lady. She was short, not unattractive, and was wearing a red outfit. She also had a handbag in one hand and a suitcase in the other. 'Good morning,' said I, 'can I help you?'

She didn't reply. Quick as a flash she shot passed me into the hallway of my flat and put her suitcase down. I turned to face her. She said, 'I've come to stay with you and the children.' I was suddenly very conscious that I was standing there wearing a dressing-gown, and nothing else. I thought; now, all I need is for this lady to start screaming and I could have a problem on my hands. Indeed, my fertile imagination was already seeing the newspaper headlines all too clearly for comfort. I picked up the suitcase and put it outside the door in the hall. I then managed to persuade her, and don't ask me how, because my brain was racing through too many possibilities to remember what I actually said, to accompany the suitcase. Having done so I leaped back inside and slammed the door. I telephoned the estate manager and he, in due course, telephoned the police.

She was only a small lady, aged I'd say, about forty, but it took two burly policemen to get her into a panda car. We later discovered that she had been a patient in a psychiatric hospital. When I spoke to her doctor it was to discover that she had, on several occasions, announced her intention of 'coming to see me and the children', but they had never really taken her seriously. I took her seriously enough to have one of those little 'spy holes' fitted in the front door. Of course, it was a no-win situation. Everyone seemed to think it was very funny, which it wasn't. The general line was 'If she'd been eighteen, and 36–24–36 I'll·bet we'd never have heard a peep out of you.'

By the autumn of 1976 the reputation the Prog had won for attracting famous names had become almost legendary and our success was generally warmly welcomed. Inevitably there was also a certain amount of jealousy but we were firmly supported by the BBC's top brass. Indeed, in high places there was good natured speculation as to which important person we would manage to 'pull' next. It was in September 1976 that Harry Walters was waiting in the foyer of Broadcasting House to greet our latest candidate for the 'hot seat'. Ian Trethowan had, by that time, been promoted from Managing Director Radio to Director General of the BBC. He walked through the front door. 'Who are you waiting for this morning, Harry?' asked the D.G.

'Oh, only Moshe Dayan, Ian,' answered Harry.

As Ian, without pause, walked on he said, 'There's no answer to that, Harry, is there?'

General Moshe Dayan had written a book called, *The Story of My Life*, and I was to interview him. My first impression was how small he was. I was also immediately aware of being in the presence of a most extraordinary man indeed. The famous black patch played its part in the first impression of course, but it was much more than that. I think it was his fantastic charm which came through most strongly. Softly spoken, extremely polite to everyone, a smile which lit up the studio, and great warmth. There were a lot of large men in Con. 'D' that day. Some were plain-clothed policemen, others had come with the official party. They appeared to have Moshe Dayan's well-being very much in mind, and seemed prepared to prove it if necessary. The notes on the dust cover of his book read: 'Dayan is one of those few men who have become a legend in their own lifetime.' It was indeed a fascinating life; archaeological expert, military strategist, political analyst. It was also a life which very nearly ended abruptly and prematurely on two separate occasions. The first was when an archaeological dig collapsed on him. The second brought about the famous black patch. It was during World War II. His unit had come under heavy fire from the Vichy French forces. Continuing in his own words, written in the book: 'I took my field glasses to try and locate the source of the shooting. I had nearly got them into focus when a rifle bullet smashed into them, splintering a lens and the metal casing, which became embedded into the socket of my left eye. I immediately lost consciousness but only for a moment. We had no painkillers with us and my head felt as if it were being pounded with sledge-hammers without stop.' He continued: 'In the Haifa hospital I asked the doctor about my condition. The doctor said: "Two things are clear. You've lost an eye, and you'll live".'

I feel that one of the perks of the job I do is that I have been privileged to meet many outstanding and fascinating people whom I would otherwise not have met. Moshe Dayan was one of them.

Another is Lord Home who had written a book called, *The Way the Wind Blows*. Again very charming, a very interesting person to interview, but it was a line in the book's sleeve notes which I found particularly endearing. As you know, he had come in for some very heavy criticism of his appearance on television. One day a make-up lady said to him, 'Of course, your problem is that you have a head like a skull.' Replied Lord Home, 'Doesn't everybody?' Squelch.

Occasionally it's quite fun to lob a small grenade in our listeners' direction and then wait and see what happens to the telephones. As for instance on the day when I interviewed a lady who said that marriage, as it is at present constituted, is completely unfair and should be done away with. No more, 'Till Death us do part'. Marriage, she said, should be substituted by a five-year agreement between the two partners, and the contract should be renewed at the end of the five-year period only if both partners wished to do so. Indignant female uproar, and one jammed BBC telephone switchboard.

Similarly, in late 1976, a lady called Esther Vilar had written a book called *The Polygamous Sex* and I interviewed her on the programme. Basically what she said, and she said it *very* basically, was that all women *really* want in a man is someone to keep them for the rest of their lives. A meal ticket was the phrase she used. Therefore, not only should a man be entitled to have more than one wife, he *ought* to, *and* he should have a mistress as well. Our lady listeners didn't like Ms Esther Vilar too much either!

As far as the BBC was concerned the big news as we moved

towards the end of November 1976 concerned Albania. The Balkan Communist state had won certain wavelength rights at an international conference a year before which meant that the BBC would have to reshuffle its network frequencies. This produced screams from just about everywhere. At the time Radio 2 was broadcasting on 1500 metres, the longwave frequency. This is a very powerful transmitter and we, on Radio 2, had a vast audience not only in the United Kingdom, but also over on the Continent and in Scandinavia. To hold, and maximize, a radio audience when they know where to find you is hard enough. To try to explain to them that you were going to move them, not just to a different frequency but also to a completely different wavelength, seemed almost impossible. The newspaper headlines didn't help.

'Radio 2 to be downgraded' thundered a headline in the *Liverpool Daily Post* of 29 November 1976.

'The powerful 1500 metre waveband is believed to be earmarked for Radio 4, the BBC's prestige news and current affairs station', said the *Dundee Courier and Advertiser*.

'Red's force Jimmy Young to move over', said the *Daily Express* in Manchester.

In the event the changes, when they came, took place extremely smoothly and Radio 2 went from strength to strength.

In January 1977 there came one of those serious interviews which nevertheless manages to produce a line funny enough to live in the memory for ever. The Union of Post Office Workers were proposing a blackout on communications between this country and South Africa, and I had arranged to interview the Union leader, Tom Jackson. I should preface the story by pointing out that Tom is just about the nicest, kindest, most sincere person you could ever wish to meet, which, of course made the line, when it popped out, all the funnier. South African politics tend to make for a pretty emotional discussion, even when one is talking to someone as eminently moderate and reasonable as Tom. So it was on 13 January 1977. The questions and answers flew thick and fast. Faster and faster in fact until, stung on some exposed nerve end by one of my questions, Tom hurled back at me, 'Ah yes, but two blacks don't make a white, do they?' Fortunately we both managed not to laugh.

Actually that was far from being the end of the 'South African boycott' story. The very next day I was interviewing John Gouriet, then Administrative Director of The National Association for Freedom, who announced that he was going to get an injunction against the Post Office Union. Later on in the month the incident was still causing a great deal of argument and I asked the Attorney General, Sam Silkin, to come in and talk to me about it, which he did. This led to another of those amusing newspaper mentions which we used to get from time to time. *The Sun*, in its leading article said, 'It's a funny old world we live in. Attorney General Sam Silkin, having staunchly refused to tell the Appeal Court his reasons for not approving the Court actions to stop the postal workers' boycott of South Africa, promptly goes on the "Jimmy Young Programme" and solemnly gives his reasons. Well done the Prog. JY for Attorney General'. If it meant I'd look as worried as Sam usually looked, I decided I wouldn't want to be Attorney General.

5-JY 'Regulars'

In January 1977 we decided to give Dr Mike Smith a run as one of our two permanent doctors on the programme, answering listeners' questions and giving medical advice. Mike had appeared before as Chief Medical Officer of the Family Planning Association, but this was his début in a more general medical role. He was immediately an enormous success.

This might be a suitable moment to write a little about our regular team of contributors, since they are people in whom our listeners always show a great deal of interest. As you will have gathered by now I am something of a fanatic about communication. So many people speak *at*, shout *at*, broadcast *at* other people without ever quite managing to get through to them. I was adamant from the start that anyone appearing on the 'JY Programme' was going to have to be able to talk *to*, and *with* other people, using good, but always understandable English. You would be surprised how few people can actually do that. Our resident team can of course, and that brings me back to Dr Mike Smith.

We have two doctors on the team who appear every other Tuesday to answer listeners' questions. They complement each other in almost every possible way, as indeed do our two lawyers, but more of that later.

Mike Smith is of medium height with sandy hair and bushy eyebrows. Piercing eyes. In matters of dress I suppose I would describe him as dapper. He sports the occasional buttonhole.

Nicely extrovert. A family man and very proud of his wife Nony and their children. He's an author, both of books and of a medical column for a women's magazine. Brightly brusque would probably describe his manner of answering listeners' questions. Always polite, but tends to 'get on with it'. Stiff upper lip. You'd imagine his prescription might be 'Brisk cold showers and the right mental attitude and you'll be as right as rain'. Nothing could be further from the truth, however, when he deals with sensitive emotional, or other problems.

Bill Dolman, our other doctor, is another cup of tea altogether. Bill is of similar physical build to Mike, not quite as broad perhaps, but there any similarity ends. Bill is your conservative dresser. He's essentially a *quiet* man. Quietly spoken, quiet mover, and the ladies, of course, absolutely love him. A widely-read man, he's also very interested in music. He studies because he likes to. Things like the law for instance. He's a JP. Also an author. He seems to put in appearances at more hospitals than I've had hot dinners. I'd say if a lady was going to have something nasty done and wanted a nice male doctor to hold her hand, Bill would get the job every time. Our William has the perfect bedside manner.

Friday, as regular listeners will know, is legal day. As with our medical team we also have two lawyers, and they alternate in dealing with legal problems which listeners send in to the programme. And again, as with our doctors, they complement each other in that they are very different personalities. Andrew Phillips is one of the newest members of the team. Having said that, one has to qualify it by pointing out that our regular contributors tend to want to stay with the programme, to such an extent that even Andrew's 'short' time with us is to be measured in years rather than months. Andrew is a big man with a big presence. His well projected voice summons up the picture of the Public School, University, and outdoor sports. Father a well-known lawyer before him, he a senior partner in his own international law firm. A sometime Liberal candidate for the European Parliament, he is now an officially adopted Liberal candidate in Lincolnshire as well. Indeed, and I know Andrew won't mind me telling the story, during the course of

ABOVE: In my studio, Continuity 'D', Broadcasting House
BELOW: Eventually, I put Uri Geller's claims to test.

LEFT: Douglas Muggeridge who encouraged me to write this book and (BELOW) Ian Trethowan who made it possible.
OPPOSITE ABOVE: Chatting with Denis Healey, the then Chancellor of the Exchequer. We discovered we had something in common.
OPPOSITE BELOW: Establishing a political balance with the then Shadow Chancellor, Robert Carr.

OPPOSITE: Doctors begin 'work to contract'. Mrs Barbara Castle confronts the doctors' spokesman, Dr Brian Lewis (ABOVE) whilst not actually meeting him on the programme – as one was being interviewed, the other listened in a separate room.

BELOW: Another guest on the programme in December 1975 was Len Murray, General Secretary of the TUC.

OPPOSITE: Newly elected Leader of the Opposition, Mrs Margaret Thatcher, stressing the importance of tackling inflation – warnings of things to come.
ABOVE: With Shirley Williams

ABOVE: A coup for the programme. An interview with Lady Falkender after Harold Wilson's resignation as Prime Minister.
BELOW: With David Steel and John Pardoe, rivals for the leadership of the Liberal Party, on 29 June 1976.
OPPOSITE: With Moshe Dayan, former Israeli Army Chief, on publication of his book

ABOVE: An interesting session with Ted Heath who drove a listener to ask, 'When are you going to stop sulking and start backing Mrs Thatcher?'
BELOW: Telling me how it should be done! Ex Prime Minister, Sir Harold Wilson joins me on the programme.
OPPOSITE: Though previously unwilling to discuss the postal workers' boycott of South Africa, Sam Silkin decided to accept my invitation to talk about it.

OPPOSITE: Out on the rounds with Eddie Straiton. Mastering a spring lamb proves more difficult than interviewing.
ABOVE LEFT: Bill Dolman, one of our doctors
ABOVE RIGHT: Mike Smith sporting his buttonhole.
BELOW: Bill Thomas, one of our lawyers, as usual in jeans and sweater, relaxing with his beagle, Robinson.

OPPOSITE: Our 'resident' vet, Eddie Straiton
ABOVE: Tony de Angeli, choosing some best buys.
BELOW: Presenting a cheque to Dr Hugh Jolly for Charing Cross Hospital from the National Medical Research Fund.

ABOVE LEFT: Andrew Phillips, our other lawyer
ABOVE RIGHT: John Carter, our best-holiday specialist
BELOW LEFT: Presenter of our gardening specials, Percy Thrower
BELOW RIGHT: JY Rugby player!

his first few appearances, there was considerable discussion between Harry and myself as to whether he was perhaps too 'up market' for us, and whether he would ever manage to settle into our legally efficient but, in the studio, more informal ways. It says much for Andrew's capacity to adapt, that he is still, very happily, with us.

In Bill Thomas, our other lawyer, who came to us before Andrew, we have the same ideal contrast in styles. Bill, like Andrew, is a tall man, though not perhaps as broad. Bespectacled. Used to have longish hair when first he began on the programme, although over the years it's become shorter. On rare occasions he'll turn up having had, very nearly, a short back and sides. Whether that's to save money by having fewer haircuts, or just to keep us on our toes I've never been quite sure. Dress – usually jeans and scruffy sweater. But occasionally turns up immaculately attired in a suit. This is usually when he's off to lecture some august body on the intricacies of the law, and if this leads you to understand that despite the deliberately casual appearance he is a first-rate lawyer, you'd be absolutely right. Bill is also the possessor of a very dry, rather off-beat sense of humour. Quite early on in his career on the programme, he and I, and eventually via the telephone the whole audience, got involved in an hilariously funny black comedy situation as to how one could get buried for free.

Bill also owns Robinson.

Robinson is a beagle, and it was in one of our early broadcasts that Bill casually informed me that Robinson has only three legs. For the strict accuracy of the record it should be pointed out that this is not absolutely true. Robinson has four legs but only three feet. I immediately fitted Robinson out with a wooden leg (the great value of radio is that nobody can see that he doesn't have one!) and Bill Thomas overnight attained fame as the Legal Beagle.

By fame I mean that *Radio Times* immediately asked whether they could take a photograph of the three-legged hound (that presented a bit of a problem as you can imagine, but we got around it). Letters of endearment, affection and sympathy flooded in for Robinson, and still do to this very day. Occasionally Bill will ramble off into some anecdote about Robinson having tummy ache, or being carsick, and the telephones are instantly red hot with doggie remedies phoned in by caring listeners.

Thursdays bring to the studio our longest-running regular contributor, Tony de Angeli. Known to our listeners, who hear the name *en passant* while hoovering, by a variety of names, Dangly, Dangle, Angelo and 'that Italian sounding name'. The name has been known to cause problems. On one occasion we had ordered a taxi to collect Tony from Broadcasting House. Tony walked down to the front door where a taxi was waiting. He and the taxi driver stared at each other off and on for ten minutes before Tony brought himself to ask whether the taxi was for him. 'No, guv, I'm picking up a lady', said the driver. A further ten minutes elapsed and Tony was getting very late for his next appointment. He again approached the driver. 'Are you sure you're not for me?' said Tony. 'No, guv' said the driver again, 'I'm here to pick up a lady. Miss Diane Jelly.'

Tony is the Editor of the influential trade magazine, *The Grocer*. He is bespectacled, witty, and has a great and bubbling sense of humour. Always laughing, he has a marvellous habit, of which I am sure he is unaware, of repeating, instantly, any funny punch line he happens to come out with. It's a kind of high adrenalin flow, action replay. He is very knowledgeable about his subject, and, indeed, many other matters as well. He is always exceptionally well briefed. And the fact that his paper commits to print the very latest information on the same day as he does our food spot is obviously a plus for the programme. Our listeners write to him with the most obscure questions on food and related matters, and he goes to endless trouble to sort out their problems for them. He has also, over the years, become the man at whom our listeners, in the nicest possible way, seem to want to hurl their tomatoes.

The price of food, of course, varies enormously throughout the length and breadth of the country. We are a programme with a vast audience which spans that whole country. Add these two things together and you will see that, as soon as Tony, in his 'best buy' section, mentions the 'average' price of something we know that is the signal for every telephone in the building to ring pointing out that where that listener lives, the price he has mentioned is anything but 'average'. Underneath it all though one senses that the listeners love him. Certainly all of us on the programme do.

In addition to our regular features we do other special programmes on a semi-regular basis and again we are very lucky in having distinguished broadcasters contributing to them.

The BBC, of course, has a considerable track record in the area of broadcasting doctors. Long before the 'JY Programme' got started on it, one distinguished broadcaster made a great impact with his instructions to 'keep your bowels open'. He was later to become Chairman of the Board of Governors of the BBC from 1967 to 1972, Charles Hill, now Baron Hill of Luton. Big oaks, as they say, from little acorns grow.

I have mentioned our regular medicos, Mike Smith and Bill Dolman. One other member of our medical team, however, is a man who contributes for us less regularly, but with just as much impact. He is the brilliant paediatrician from Charing Cross Hospital, Dr Hugh Jolly. Hugh, like Bill Dolman, is possessed of the perfect bedside manner. Tall, slightly stooped, bespectacled, he looks every inch the studious academician that he is. He also has the absolutely essential ability to convey complicated answers to a non-medical audience in a manner, and in language, which they understand completely. This is not to say that he glosses over problems. On the contrary, if a listener has written in with a problem which Hugh considers so serious that in his opinion it requires immediate attention from the family doctor, or from a specialist, he will say so, and in no uncertain terms. On many occasions he is able to explain to people why their fears for their own health or the health of their loved ones are groundless, but he can also often be controversial. Not all mothers or fathers listening, nor indeed doctors for that matter, agree with everything he says. I don't think he would expect them to. But he will always give his views sensibly and calmly, and he seems able to convince his audience of the soundness of what he is saying.

A little while ago, Hugh asked me if I would address the West London Medico-Chirurgical Society. I was flattered and terrified at one and the same time. 'What do you want me to talk to them about?' said I.

'Communication', said he. 'It's as big a problem in medicine as it is in many other areas in life, and that's one thing you do know about.'

Oddly enough, for me, the most interesting thing was what followed the talk I gave.

Hugh asked me if I would like to go upstairs and see around the wards, of which he is in charge. I said I should love to. We tiptoed quietly through the darkened adult wards. All the patients were in bed and asleep. Ahead of us I could see lights. As we approached I could also hear voices, children's voices. Then children's laughter. We entered a brightly-lit ward. There were children all over the place, some were asleep, some were sitting up in bed, some were just walking about. As also were a few adults. Half a dozen were watching the television. They ignored us as we walked in, intent on the box. Three children were clustered around a bed in which another one was sitting. One of the three was taking his pulse. Hugh walked over and talked to them. They explained their symptoms and how they were feeling. The whole atmosphere was relaxed, free and easy. No fear of the doctor. No standing on ceremony. Parents walked in and out of the ward. In cases where it was felt that the parent staying in the ward would benefit the child, that arrangement was made. He explained to parents that the hospital didn't have beds to spare to accommodate them, but that if they didn't mind sleeping on portable beds by their child's bed or in the play room, then that would be perfectly in order.

Parents stopped and talked naturally with other people's children. Nurses walked quietly through wards and paused to chat here and there. It may be that other hospitals practise the same ideas of course, but certainly I had never seen anything like it. Hugh told me that getting rid of the old style stiffness of approach made the children so much more relaxed that, when they came to have operations, or treatment of any kind, things were much easier for both patients and staff. As for children watching television at that hour of the night, said Hugh, 'When they're tired they'll go to bed. What's more they'll sleep well through the night.' As Hugh talked, I walked and looked around. Everything seemed very much like the man himself. Eminently sensible.

Other special programmes which we undertake involve the nationalized industries. On a fairly regular basis we invite the various chairmen to come into the studio and deal with our listeners' problems, and believe me, we are never short of problems for them to have a go at. Naturally, they vary greatly in their ability to communicate with the public. And, one has to say, they also vary in their desire to get involved with the public. The good ones, though, really are very, very good.

A name that springs readily to mind is Sir William Barlow, when he was Chairman of the Post Office.

Bill Barlow's method, when confronted with a listener's problem which, in his opinion, should have received attention some time ago was simple. He would say, on the air and direct to the listener, 'You will hear from me about this matter within forty-eight hours.' I must confess that, the first time he said it, I and my sceptical research team tended to think, we'll believe *that* when we see it, but he never failed us. We knew he'd carried out his promise when we received the letters of thanks from listeners for getting problems sorted out when they had completely failed to get any action. You may well say that there should be no necessity for a 'Jimmy Young Programme' to provoke action being taken about complaints. Action should be taken anyway. Absolutely right of course, there can be no argument about that. The fact is though, that, as we all know, things can get into a tangle and, when we have been able to shake up officialdom and get something done for our listeners, that has always given us the very greatest satisfaction.

The programme content is not always heavy of course. John Carter, another author and broadcaster, whom you may have seen on the 'Holiday Programme' on BBC Television, comes in to give our listeners the very best holiday advice and suggestions. Then there are our Gardening Specials with Percy Thrower. The BBC allowing us to use Percy as our gardening expert gave me particular satisfaction. I had, of course, seen Percy on television and heard him on radio many times over the years, and to me he has always seemed, without any doubt, the number one authority on gardening. He has such knowledge of his subject, and such an excellent manner of communicating his knowledge. If there is such a thing as a gardening bedside manner then Percy, in my opinion, has it. However, at the time when we proposed to begin our Gardening Specials, Percy and the BBC were having, how shall I put it, a slight disagreement. Doubt was expressed to me as to whether his appointment as our gardening expert would meet with approval. Anyway, Harry and I decided to go ahead and put Percy's name forward, and to our delight, he was accepted.

He is an absolute joy to work with. I speak as someone who knows nothing at all about gardening, but I'll tell you one thing, I could listen to Percy for hours. His love of the countryside and all things that grow in it comes shining through in every word that he speaks, and there is nothing he doesn't know about his subject. He is never at a loss on how to answer any question phoned in by a listener and he doesn't need to 'look it up' first.

It would be invidious, and also impossible, to attempt to pick out the most popular of our special contributors. However, if there were a league table, one man who would be well up towards the top would be our 'pet vet', Eddie Straiton.

It's almost impossible to know where to start to write about Eddie. I suppose a thumbnail description would go like this: an ever smiling, short, stocky Scot who's built like a brick outhouse. Or a very hard Rugby League scrum half. In fact he's not a rugby player. He was a very gifted amateur, almost a professional, Scottish soccer player. He's one of the fittest men I've ever met in my life. I'm not joking when I say that he goes to Majorca on holiday, and relaxes by running up steep hills in Army boots before breakfast. He drives an open sports car whatever the weather, and is always the picture of pink, wind-tanned health, from his daily exposure to the elements. He has a handshake like a vice. He also has one of the readiest, and least inhibited senses of humour. A great raconteur and after-dinner speaker, he can sometimes get himself into hot water as happened with the cat spaying story. He is, and I know the whole team would agree with me, one of the warmest hearted, kindest men one could ever wish to meet. Indeed, his generosity, and his willingness to fight for the underdog has often got him into trouble. Usually when it wasn't even his own fight in the first place. I don't think he would mind, indeed I think he'd be rather proud, if I said that he is, by nature, a bit of a rebel.

When Eddie first began broadcasting for us, never having met him before, I was naturally a little apprehensive as to how good or otherwise he might turn out to be. What I had not realized was that he had helped to launch the farming television programmes in the Midlands many, many years ago. He is a man of vast experience in the art of broadcasting communication, as I was to realize as soon as I opened the mike and he got cracking. Eddie, like Percy Thrower, is another man who doesn't want, or need, to see the listeners' questions in advance. Indeed they both actively prefer *not* to see them. Their view, and I absolutely agree with them, is that provided a person really knows what he's talking about, you get better, and more spontaneous, answers when they come right off the top of the head. My boast on the programme, on Eddie's behalf, is that listeners can send him in any question about any kind of animal, either farm or pet, and he will not be stumped for an answer. I must say though that I thought I had him on one occasion when I picked up a listener's question which asked what was the incubation period for hatching a tortoise egg. I didn't. As I might have guessed, he knew the answer: twenty years.

One of his most famous television appearances was on a farming programme. He was campaigning for the greater use of anaesthetics. The argument warmed up and, at one stage in the proceedings, Eddie was seen chasing his National Farmers Union opponent around the studio waving a giant castrating iron. Eddie won the debate.

Author and vet, James Herriott, and Eddie went to college together, and they are still great friends. Their careers have intertwined to the extent that, while it was the Herriott books which supplied the raw material for the television series 'All Creatures Great and Small', Eddie was actually the veterinary adviser on the series, and his were the hands seen in shot when any veterinary work was required to be done on screen. Indeed Eddie is no mean author himself; his own books are big sellers in thirteen different languages.

Perhaps I might indulge myself with a personal Eddie Straiton anecdote. I had been rather ill and Eddie invited me to spend a couple of days at his cottage in the Staffordshire countryside. He also asked me whether I would like to accompany him on his rounds, which I said I would love to do. Day one and his lovely, and most efficient, secretary, Penny, collected me early in the morning to drive into the Veterinary Hospital, some ten miles away. The weather was foul, thick, driving snow. We arrived at the hospital and Eddie promptly began to kit me out. On went a tartan lumber jacket. 'I was given that by a grave digger', said Eddie. Thick socks went on over my own socks, and then wellington boots a couple of sizes too big. On top of the whole thing went a zip-up Alfa Romeo rally outfit, topped off with an Alfa Romeo hat. A sight to be seen, I can tell you. We went out into the yard to drive off on Eddie's round. Outside stood two Alfa Romeos: the saloon, in which Penny and I had arrived, and an Alfa Spyder sports car with the roof down. I made for the saloon. 'Where do you think you're going?' asked Eddie.

'To the car', says I.

'I never travel in a closed car,' said Eddie, 'whatever the weather.'

'But it's snowing', I protested.

'Sit down low in the passenger seat,' advised Eddie, 'and it'll go over the top of your head.'

Intensive care unit, here I come, I thought. And I hadn't even seen Eddie drive yet. He does that by the simple expedient of putting his right foot flat on the floor and keeping it there. I quite thought my last moment had come. I sank lower and lower in the passenger seat, braced my feet against the bulkhead, and prayed. We never hit a thing. I ended up, among other things, holding a tin of liquid paraffin at the business end of a calf while Eddie gave it an enema. I came back glowing with health, having had the time of my life. Quite a character is our Eddie.

6-Live from Moscow

The year 1977 was to be a very special one for the 'JY Prog'. We were to make history by becoming the first BBC Radio programme to be beamed 'live' to Europe from the Soviet Union. Oddly enough the story actually began way back in 1972. I was then still on Radio 1, and my producer, Doreen Davies, and I came up with the suggestion of taking the programme to Moscow. Once the laughter had died down and management saw that we were really serious, we were given the go-ahead to try. Accordingly, we approached the Soviet Embassy. The Russians tend not to be the swiftest movers in the world, and, after a long wait, we were informed that someone from the Embassy would be prepared to come along and take a look at the Prog in action. In due course, two Russian gentlemen turned up at Broadcasting House. They were the Russian equivalent of the 'hard' and 'soft' man team one hears about in police investigations. The hard man was short and almost as wide as he was tall. He spoke no English. At least he said he didn't. We were never absolutely convinced about that. The soft man looked to be straight out of the Savoy Grill, complete with smart blazer, cavalry twill trousers and suede shoes. He, of course, spoke fluent English. They sat, impassively, through the entire programme and then departed, clutching the taped recordings we had made for them. We never heard from them again. The project disappeared as though submerged under a gigantic Russian snowstorm.

However, time passed and, late in 1976, I suggested that we should have another try to achieve what would, after all, be a 'first' for broadcasting. We again approached the Russians and, somewhat to our surprise, they agreed to come along and discuss it. The talks went well, indeed there was really only one fundamental area of disagreement, and that was over the programmes being 'live'. As I have explained earlier in the book we try to make everything on the programme live, and we certainly had no intention of altering that for the Russians. However, every time we referred to our programme being 'live' we were headed off. 'Yes, we quite understand,' the Russians would say, 'you mean you record your interviews the day before and then transmit them live the following day.'

'No,' we would patiently explain, 'we mean that we sit there, in the studio, with the guests, and the interviews are actually transmitted as we are doing them, live.'

One could see the worry clearly enough. Western broadcaster sitting in Moscow studio, and, if it's live, there's no chance of getting the scissors into the tape, is there? But, that was the only way we were going to do the broadcasts and, in the end, by being polite but firm, we won. The broadcasting dates were set for 16 and 17 May 1977 and we all knew that, at last, one of the really great radio adventures was under way.

When the news was announced in February, the Press, of course, had a field day. 'It's the Jimmy Young Showski', 'JY Prog Goes Red', 'Listen in to Comrade Jimmy', 'Orft We Jolly Well Goski', 'The JY Prog Steppes into Radio History', were just some of the newspaper headlines.

Our own view was summed up by the man who would be leading the team going to Moscow, Charles McLelland, then Controller of Radios 1 and 2. Charles said, 'This is a broadcasting scoop, and naturally we are proud of that.' Of course one's public and private faces do not always wear exactly the same expression. Publicly the whole team were euphoric at having pulled off something which many people had thought to be impossible. Privately, however, I occasionally awoke, sweating, at 2 a.m. wondering exactly what we had landed ourselves with. True, man could broadcast from the moon to the earth, so there was no logical reason why he shouldn't be able to broadcast live from Moscow to Europe. Nonetheless, it had never been done by the BBC, and there must always be an element of risk in any 'first', however much care and planning is put into it. Certainly in as much as one could plan ahead we would. A research team would visit Moscow well in advance to look in detail at studios, equipment, accommodation and technical facilities; to confer with the broadcasting authorities and to meet the guests to whom we proposed to talk. There was an enormous amount of work to do and, since the broadcast dates were less than three months away, not a great deal of time in which to do it.

Also, we are not a large team and, in spite of the glamour and excitement of possibly creating a small slice of history, there was still the pressure of day to day broadcasting with which to cope.

On Tuesday 5 April 1977 I heard what I have always thought to be the beginning of the end of the fabulously successful 'Starsky and Hutch' television series. It all began innocently enough. The producer of the series, Joe Naar, was in London, and we had suggested that he might like to pop into the studio and be interviewed. During the course of our chat, Joe mentioned that he proposed to change the format of the show for the next series. 'Why do that to such a successful series?' I asked. He told me that the show had been subjected to tremendous pressure in America from certain groups who said it was too violent. True to say, the Annan Committee in this country had also named 'Starsky and Hutch' and 'The Sweeney' as series which 'made the hours when they are on some of the most violent on British TV.'

I have to say that I had never thought 'Starsky and Hutch' to be particularly violent. Certainly not when one considers what Jimmy Cagney used to get up to in some of his films, now being shown on television. I asked Joe what he thought would be the result of this change in policy. He said, 'Well if you want an educated guess, I would say the show will not be as popular in future.' Certainly our listeners seemed to agree. Protest calls poured into the BBC switchboard. The theme of most of them seemed to be that it was *real life* violence which they found upsetting, not violence which they knew was only acting. 'Cut out the showing of real life violence like the clubbing of seal cubs', they said. I was very much afraid that Joe's 'educated guess' was going to prove to be correct, and it seems that it has.

One way and another, and quite unintentionally, we seemed to be having a 'violence week'. Two days after talking to Joe Naar, I was interviewing a lady from the *Nursing Times* on the subject of violence against nurses in hospital casualty departments. On the very same morning I interviewed the Minister of State for Sport, and the manager of Manchester United, Denis Howell and Tommy Docherty, about soccer hooligans. It's often a quite amusing little game for us on the team to predict in advance what our listeners' reaction will be to any given subject: for instance, soccer hooligans. That, of course, was one of our easier predictions. Gone were the peace-loving telephone calls of Tuesday to 'cut out real-life violence'. The BBC switchboard lit up and in flooded, 'Birch them'; 'Put 'em in the stocks and throw things at 'em'; 'Tattoo their foreheads, "I am a soccer hooligan"'; 'Shave their heads'. I am in no way expressing a personal opinion but, after many years of doing my radio programme, there is one thing of which I am absolutely certain: if a countrywide referendum were carried out, capital punishment probably, and corporal punishment certainly, would have been back in being as the law of the land a very long time ago.

We were all very much aware that every day that passed brought us one day nearer to our trip to the Soviet Union. The adrenalin flowed, but the butterflies fluttered as well.

On the other side of the Iron Curtain all seemed perfectly well. Indeed the Russians had asked whether we would like to extend our trip from two days to four. They were suggesting now that perhaps we would like to do two programmes from Moscow, and follow them up with two more from Leningrad. It sounded exciting. Two 'firsts' instead of one. But, having talked it over, we decided not to push our luck too far and to settle, on this occasion at any rate, for just two programmes from Moscow.

John Gurnett, the programme's chief researcher, and Alan Wilson, one of the two engineering experts who would be going with us, had already flown to Moscow to 'do a recce'. We try never to leave anything to chance. Alan reported that, so far as he could tell, there was no reason at all why it shouldn't work technically. John Gurnett said he had talked with the broadcasting authorities who seemed very helpful, and also with the proposed guests who seemed quite willing to talk. He reported that they didn't appear to have been warned as to what they could or could not say, and seemed unworried about going 'live'. John had also come back with one additional bit of information, which was to prove invaluable; it took him no time at all to see that there are queues for, literally, everything in Moscow. To his great credit it also took him no time at all to find a way around that particular problem. On his return to London from the 'recce' trip he outlined both the problem, and the solution. 'Tights, chewing gum and heavy rock LPs,' said John, 'that's what you need to get by in Moscow.' And so it proved, although we were still some weeks away from discovering that.

What I *had* discovered, it must have been mentioned in conversation many times but had never registered with me before, was that we were flying on Friday, the 13th.

John Gurnett, Harry Walters, and Alan Wilson, had already flown ahead on Wednesday so the party which was to fly on Friday consisted of Charles McLelland, Controller Radio 2, Geoffrey Owen, Head of Radio 2, engineer John Ford, researcher Mike Rhodes, secretary Liz Sugden and myself.

Since, as the whole world knows, everyone is equal in the Soviet Union one would be justified in thinking that they would have only one class of accommodation on their passenger aircraft. Not so, they have first class and economy, like all other countries' airlines. The BBC therefore, being the budget-conscious organization they are, had decided that, to save expense, three of the party should fly first class, and the other six would fly economy. We arrived at Heathrow at 2 p.m. for a 2.50 take off, and were met there by the Aeroflot representative. I expected to see a female commissar. On the contrary, she turned out to be an absolutely delightful, charming, softly spoken north country lady who had never been to Russia in her life. She also had a very pleasant surprise to spring on us. The Russians, perhaps feeling a twinge of pity that the BBC was so hard up, had, for no extra charge, upgraded the whole party to first class. If it was a Communist plot to make a good impression it certainly succeeded.

Even before we had boarded the plane to Moscow, there had been some sniping at the venture in the Press. Pressure groups of various kinds had written letters to the papers suggesting that we would be 'used as a propaganda exercise by the Russians'. For our part, we had gone out of our way to ensure that this could not possibly happen. We had, for instance, mounted a special broadcast in London on Thursday 19 May featuring Lord Chalfont and David Simpson of Amnesty International so that, if there *was* any unintentional bias during the Moscow broadcasts, there would be an opportunity for someone to put the other side of the story. We had done everything in our power to ensure a proper balance. However, I knew that, unless the broadcasts were a total success, and seen to be so, we would come under enormous fire.

As we sat at the end of the runway, awaiting clearance for take-off, our thoughts were interrupted by the voice of a young Russian air hostess. 'What would you like to drink when we are airborne?' she asked.

'What do you suggest?' we said.

'The champagne cocktails are rather good', said she.

Not a wheel had turned and already I had received two shocks. First and second class travel in the classless society, and now the recommendation to enjoy the ultimate in capitalist drinks aboard a Communist aircraft. I have to say, incidentally, that when the champagne cocktails arrived our air hostess most certainly had not exaggerated. They were excellent. They were also extremely potent. A couple of those and you really knew you'd had a drink. And since we'd kindly been upgraded to first class they were free, which was even better.

I half-heartedly began to speculate as to whether I was on the right side of the Iron Curtain, but any such thoughts were speedily banished on arrival at Moscow. The magnificent hospitality ended when the flight ended.

All airports suffer from an excess of red tape, everybody knows that. However, until you've seen the Moscow airport brand of red tape you ain't seen nothing. Quite literally, everything has to be accounted for. I've never seen as much form filling in my life. Every penny you take in must be noted. When you come out again you account for what you've spent, say what you've got left, and if your accounts don't balance you don't get out until they do.

We had the advantage of being met by John and Harry. As an official BBC party we had also been allocated a Russian 'guide' but even with the help of the three of them I thought we'd never get things sorted out. Eventually of course, tired and short tempered, we set off for our Moscow hotel in a kind of mini bus.

On the way, we passed something which, to me, seemed highly significant when trying to understand the suspicion of foreigners which lurks in the Soviet mind. It was a tank trap, marking the spot where the German army ground to a halt in its advance into Russia, and it is now preserved for ever as a war memorial. It is very close indeed to the City of Moscow and is a grim reminder of how close the Germans came to winning the war.

During the short time we were in Moscow I found it depressing to realize how very important to the Russian authorities is this keeping alive of war memories. Indoctrination begins early. As you walk about Red Square you see the parties of young school-children being taken to view the tomb of the Unknown Soldier. One got the impression that, although the war had ended over thirty years ago, the Russian leadership is terrified lest a generation should grow up and say, 'Isn't it about time we forgave and forgot?'

We duly arrived at the Rossia Hotel, No. 6 Razin Street, Moscow. It is enormous. So huge, in fact, that one day, when the whole of our party had been out, we walked back to the hotel to discover that we were passing a side entrance. Thinking we would avoid the long trek around to the front entrance by cutting through, we went in. But the place is so vast that within minutes we were hopelessly lost, had to edge our way back outside, wander around to the front entrance, and start all over again. When you book in you are given a pass. Our guide, Uri, stressed to us the importance of that little piece of paper. You show it to the gentleman at the main door in order to get out. And, should you lose it while you are out, you don't get back in again. It's as simple as that. You also, of course, get a key. And a key lady. Key ladies are, as the Americans would put it, something else again. At the end of each floor of bedrooms between you and the lifts towards which you are heading, sits a key lady. As you go out you hand her your key. As you come in you show her your pass, and she gives you your key. No pass, no key. Life is basic and simple in the Soviet Union. Key ladies, so far as we could judge, came in one-size packages. They were all very short, very fat, and they all wore very scanty mini skirts. When bending down to pick up a dropped key, they were not a pretty sight. They also listen in to your telephone conversations, or so we were told. I am sure this is not true, of course, which is a polite way of saying that I'm *not* sure it's not true.

So many odd things happen in Moscow that one is never certain where facts end and fantasies begin. For instance, there were nine of us in our party. We were an official BBC party, invited by the Soviet broadcasting authorities. You would assume they knew that we would have a great deal of work to do while we were there, and that they would therefore make arrangements for our rooms to be in close proximity to each other. In fact we were all booked into rooms on different floors of the hotel. Life could not possibly have been made more difficult for us had it been done intentionally. At a time like this, one tries to convince oneself that it was probably just slack organization. Yet, it's bound to set you wondering. And it did.

We had agreed, since those of us who had travelled that day were feeling rather tired, to meet downstairs in the dining-room, have an early dinner and go off to bed. As we approached the dining-room we could hear music playing and we realized that we had stumbled upon the Russian equivalent of the Friday night dinner-dance. It was rather like being put into a time machine and swept back forty years or so to some bourgeois *thé dansant*. The whole atmosphere was one of faded gentility. The band, on a raised dais, played dated arrangements rather badly. A blonde lady was singing standard songs off key. It was like a well-intentioned, but badly-executed, attempt to re-create something which had faded into history many years ago, or perhaps a satirical comment in a film by a young *avant-garde* film director. Eventually we were seated and handed a large menu. We waded through it with great difficulty. We need not have bothered. Almost everything was 'off' anyway. Waiters bustled by at great speed, but it seemed they always bustled *by*. Nobody ever offered to stop. Every time we attempted to attract a waiter's attention we were acknowledged with a brief, brusque, *niet*. The atmosphere of Aeroflot, champagne cocktails and well-chosen menus was clearly long gone; possibly only to return on the way home, if then. Eventually we ate. But as we made our way to our rooms we reflected that, if our stomachs were going to survive Moscow, it would be necessary to play our ace: John's records, chewing gum and tights.

On Saturday morning we had arranged to visit the Radio Station to have a look at the studio in which we were to work. We were somewhat taken aback to discover that, in contrast to my tiny, intimate, homely Continuity studio in London's Broadcasting House, this studio was absolutely vast, complete with large grand piano standing in one corner. John Ford and Alan Wilson were there to assure us that as far as they were concerned, technically that is, they could make it work. Clearly, as far as atmosphere and ambiance were concerned, that was going to be all down to me on the night. Our Russian hosts agreed to arrange some screens around me to give me a smaller working area.

On Saturday afternoon I gave a couple of press interviews, and then came the moment which was to change our eating habits, and those of a few British people whom we had yet to meet. I was walking quietly about the hotel looking for some way to put John Gurnett's assets to practical use. The trouble was, everybody I approached spoke no English at all. I was passing a restaurant when I saw a lady cleaning up the tables inside. She was blonde and, in her younger days, had clearly been very attractive. For the umpteenth time that day I asked, 'Excuse me, but do you speak English?'

In halting English, and very slowly, she said, 'Only a little.' That was enough.

'We have some tights and chewing gum if you would like them', I said. It was like winning the pools. For both of us.

'I would like please,' she said, 'my son loves chewing gum. I need tights.'

'May we have a table for nine for breakfast tomorrow?' said I. 'If we could have something like eggs and bacon that would be lovely.' I reported the breakthrough to the team, and we waited to see what tomorrow would bring. At least it couldn't be worse than it had been so far.

Saturday evening brought a parting of the ways for us. Everyone, with the exception of John Gurnett and myself, was going to the circus. I have never been particularly interested in the circus, but I was extremely interested in talking to the man with whom John and I were going to have a meal. His name is Vladimir Pozner. Vladimir's father went to America to work when Vladimir was very young, and the family lived there for twenty years. Therefore, while thinking like a Russian, Vladimir speaks English like an American. I was very keen to meet him, because he was one of the people I was due to interview, and I had the feeling that he might well turn out to be a formidable broadcasting opponent. You do not have to be in the Soviet Union very long to realize how very important status is. A senior member of our party had impressed upon us at a meeting in London, 'It is vitally important that the Russians respect you.' It was quite obvious that the Russian authorities respected Vladimir.

He had a four-room apartment and you don't come by four room apartments all that easily in Moscow. He offered us a wide range of drinks and hard-to-obtain records played in the background. We spent a very pleasant evening. On the way home I thought to myself: I reckon Vladimir's in the Moscow first team.

Breakfast on Sunday morning was quite an occasion. We all turned up on time, and sure enough there was our blonde waitress friend waiting for us. John discreetly slipped her the goodies, and we sat expectantly. I cannot in all honesty say that what we got was the best egg and bacon I've ever had in my life. It was a skillet full of something yellow, in which one could see tiny flecks of something which looked vaguely like bacon. However, it was hot and, provided one ate enough of the excellent Russian bread with it, it was also filling. We tucked in. While we were doing so, I saw a hand waving at me at one of the tables half-way down this very large restaurant. Wondering who on earth the Russian thought he was gesturing to, I waved back. Immediately a man got to his feet and approached our table. He wasn't a Russian at all. He was a Brit with a Massey Ferguson delegation to Moscow. Not only had they failed to get anything to eat but they were still failing. 'I don't know how you've done it Jim, but do you think we could join your table please?' he said. Next day we picked up a delegation from Girling Brakes as well. There's nothing like sound research I always say.

The highlight of our Moscow Sunday morning was a visit to the British Embassy, where we were warmly greeted by the British Ambassador and our special contact there, the man who had done so much to smooth our visit, the Cultural Attaché, William (known to all as Bill) Marsden. Yes, believe it or not, the 'JY Prog' visit had been dubbed by the Russians, a 'Cultural Visit'. The British Embassy is actually a very lovely building indeed, but getting in to discover that fact is not easy. It involves much pass showing, and close scrutiny by large, armed Russian soldiers who goose step purposefully up and down outside the front entrance. Eventually, after much of the red tape so beloved of Moscow, we were allowed in. We were shown over the building, and our guide indicated the room in the basement which he said, jokingly, was the only room in the entire building in which you could be sure of having an unbugged conversation. As I've said earlier, quite a lot of 'joking' conversation goes on in Moscow about bugging, monitoring, surveillance and so on and, as a visitor for only a brief time, I was never quite certain where the joking ended and reality began. We took drinks with our hosts on the Embassy terrace, which affords an excellent view of the Kremlin. For some reason best known to himself, this used to infuriate Stalin. He tried for years to get the British to agree to move to another building, which they steadfastly refused to do. Most likely because they were happy where they were. I'm sure it couldn't possibly have been because the knowledge that it annoyed Stalin appealed to their British sense of humour.

On Sunday afternoon we met the guests I was to be interviewing during the next two days. Then it was home to the hotel to do some last minute preparations, and off to bed.

Monday 16 May. This, then, was it. The first of two BBC history-making days. The Monday programme was to cover housing, women's role in society, young people, juvenile crime, sport, with former Wimbledon tennis star Anna Dmitrieva, and, of course, dissidents, human rights and emigration. A formidable package. The next morning the London *Times* reported, 'Yesterday, Jimmy Young, the British broadcaster, sat in a red-carpeted studio in central Moscow and conducted the first live radio chat show to be transmitted from East to West. For the Soviet state radio and television committee it was an unprecedented experiment.'

On the same day the *Guardian* said, 'The Iron Curtain turned briefly into a sieve yesterday as a jolly Russian journalist called Vladimir Pozner chatted to Jimmy Young for all the world as though the K.G.B. were asleep. He galloped into the controversial fields where Jim was tip-toeing and launched into a carefree admission of Russian social problems.'

'"Did Soviet teenagers engage in truancy, alcoholism, vandalism, the generation gap and living together?" asked Jim. "Of course they do", said Vladimir, "Of course there's truancy, and of course we have a Soviet alcoholic problem".'

The *Daily Mirror* said, 'There were plenty of sniggers when it was announced that Jimmy Young would present the first 'Live' radio show from Moscow. What could he do? But, in a Russian word, yesterday's programme was "Khorosho" – excellent. Jimmy put some straight questions to Vladimir Pozner, a smooth-talking Moscow broadcaster. And pinned him down to admitting that there *is* Anti-Semitism in Russia.'

I breathed a sigh of relief. The first programme had been judged a success. The *Morning Star* described me as being 'sweat stained but pleased'. Little did I know how much the atmosphere in the studio would have changed by the following morning.

For the moment, however, all was peace and light. Our Russian hosts had laid on a little reception for us, and we were to return the compliment after the second programme on the following day. We went into the reception feeling exhausted, but happy.

The champagne cocktails were disappearing at a rate of knots, and Mr Lev Korolev, the head of the Foreign Relations Department at the Soviet State Committee for Broadcasting, who spoke no English, was talking to me through an interpreter. Mr Korolev's face looks as though it has been carved from granite. However, it was breaking into what seemed as though it might become a smile, given a couple of thousand years to mature.

The interpreter told me, 'Mr Korolev says he thinks you are an excellent broadcaster.' I thanked him.

Korolev then rattled off in Russian, at some length, to the interpreter. At the end of the flurry of words his shoulders heaved like a Russian Ted Heath, and his face managed the briefest of smiles. The interpreter turned to me and translated. 'Mr Korolev says that, if tomorrow's broadcast goes as well as today's, he would like you to come back and do some broadcasts from Siberia. He says, "Tell Mr Young we will send him to Siberia, but not for ever."' Mr Korolev was not to be as friendly the following day. That evening we were taken out to dinner by our Russian hosts, and I was again brought face to face with an aspect of Russian life which I intensely disliked. As I've mentioned earlier there are queues for just about everything in Moscow, and that included the restaurant to which we were being taken. However, we were swept imperiously past the queue, straight into the restaurant itself, and immediately seated. The Muscovites, of course, were still shivering in the cold outside. Our Russian hosts would probably say that they were merely being courteous to their guests.

Tuesday morning dawned and we set off for the Radio Station in an altogether more confident mood. After all we had already had a big success the previous day. The BBC had reported to us on the telephone a 'tremendous response from listeners.' We had had the Tuesday morning British Press reports read to us which, overall, were excellent. And, of course, we knew the Russians were happy because they had told us so. We walked jauntily into the studio. It was rather like walking into a refrigerator.

We were met by sullen faces. No one spoke. It was all very embarrassing, not to mention perplexing, because we couldn't for the life of us think why. Until, that is, Vladimir Pozner arrived. He looked absolutely terrible. His face was white and drawn. He had dark rings under his eyes. I went over to him. I said, 'You look bloody awful, what's the matter?'

He said, 'It was the broadcast, wasn't it. I've been on the carpet.'

'But they loved the broadcast.' I said, 'They told us so.'

'No, not that broadcast,' said Vladimir, 'the one the BBC beamed back to the Soviet Union last night.'

I should perhaps explain that the two broadcasts I was doing from Moscow, although going live to Europe, were not being transmitted in the Soviet Union. However, the BBC External Services, which, among other things, broadcasts programmes to Communist bloc countries, had decided otherwise. Without telling us, they had recorded my Monday morning transmission from Moscow. They then selected all the 'heaviest' bits, and beamed them back into the Soviet Union on the Monday night. Completely unbeknown to us therefore, the juiciest parts of the programme which the Soviet government had never intended Soviet citizens to hear, had already found their way back into the Soviet Union. What is more, we had decided, even before we had arrived in Moscow, that although the Monday programme would be a probing one, the final one on Tuesday would be even more so. There was no way, therefore, in which I could do anything other than the firm, questioning programmes we had gone there to do. I told Vladimir so.

To his credit, since I've no doubt that 'being on the carpet' in the Soviet Union is a considerably harsher experience than it is in Britain, he said, 'Don't worry about me, I'll be OK. You just carry on and do your job.' And this I did.

The most interesting experience, however, was to come *after* the Tuesday programme.

In Britain, *The Sun* newspaper announced 'Jim's radio show starts cold war again.' In response to the Russians' hospitality after the first programme we had arranged our own little reception for them on the Tuesday. I had the misfortune to be one of the first of the British party to arrive. Standing at the bar was an agitated group of Russians. Just about the most agitated was Mr Korolev.

I went over to get a drink. Within two seconds Mr Korolev was poking me in the chest with a very large, stiff, Russian forefinger. Through the interpreter I asked what was wrong, as though I didn't know. Sure enough, it was the broadcast of the night before which, by now, seemed to have involved the British Embassy in Moscow, the Foreign Office in London, and was developing into a major row. I tried to tell him that BBC External Services are distinct from the domestic service for which we worked. Explaining that to someone in Britain is difficult enough. Explaining it in Moscow to a non-English speaking Russian through an interpreter – no chance. I decided to take the soft (is cowardly the word I'm looking for?) line.

'Tell Mr Korolev,' I told the interpreter 'when we come back to broadcast from Siberia, I'm sure all will be peace and light.'

Angry Russian phrases flowed from Mr Korolev, and his arm moved forward and backward, horizontally. Replied the interpreter, 'Mr Korolev says, any more broadcasts like last night and today, and we shall *all* be in Siberia, *sawing.*'

I, for one, felt a long way from home. However, I realized that, if there were any people who thought we were going to be 'used' by the Russians, and there were, they had been shown in the clearest possible way, by our hosts, that they had been totally wrong.

The Russians, however, still had one surprise in store. The next day we were waiting in the hotel foyer for the airport bus when a very distraught key lady burst out of the lift and headed for our party. She shouted animatedly at our guide, Uri. She was clearly most distressed. Her arms were flailing wildly, but when they chanced to point they levelled in the general direction of John Gurnett.

Uri walked over to John. 'You don't happen to have one of the Hotel's coat hangers in your case, do you?' 'Would you open your luggage please?' This poor old John was forced to do in the middle of the crowded hotel foyer. To this day he swears that it was an accident, that in his haste to pack he swept up all his coat hangers into a heap which he just dumped in to his case. Having seen the evidence one would have to believe him. For there, lying right on top of the clothes was the cheapest, nastiest, white plastic coat hanger you would ever wish not to see. To the key lady however it was clear evidence of a deep-laid capitalist plot. She seized it triumphantly and proceeded to poke John in the chest with it until made to desist by Uri. Quick as a flash John trumped her ace by whipping out his last pair of tights and, with a beaming smile, presented them to her in the middle of the crowded foyer. Pink and flustered, but happy, she fled. Only later did we find out that key ladies' orders are to count the hangers before you leave the hotel. If there's one missing you don't check out. As we had just discovered.

I cannot say I was sorry to leave. True, we had done two successful programmes. True, we had made a little broadcasting history, but, after take-off, when I heard the thud as the landing gear came up and I knew we were really on our way home, I felt a great sense of relief.

Oddly enough the end of the story, at any rate as far as my part in it was concerned, didn't come until a couple of years later. I was being interviewed by Tony Lewis at Pebble Mill in Birmingham for 'Saturday Night at the Mill'. We were talking about the Moscow broadcasts when Tony told me a story. He said, 'You know, I had the privilege of doing the *second* live broadcast for the BBC from Moscow. I went there just about a month after you had left.' He went on, 'The Russians were showing us around the Radio Station and asked whether I would like to see the studio from which I was going to broadcast. I said I would. As they showed me in to the studio the Russian guide said proudly, "This is it Mr Lewis. *This* is the Jimmy Young studio"!'

So perhaps we may yet be welcomed back one of these days after all.

7-Radio 2 at Ten

Norman St John-Stevas came in to talk to me about parental attitudes to school on Tuesday 26 July 1977. I mention this fact not because there was anything remarkable about it, but because of an amusing little bit of one upmanship, reported in Hansard. Norman returned to the House to take part in a debate about the quality, or lack of quality, depending on one's point of view, of certain BBC programmes. Shirley Williams was Secretary of State for Education and Science at the time, and she was also taking part. Said Norman to the House, 'Will the Secretary of State make clear that she does not agree with the view that all pop music programmes are moronic and contribute to illiteracy? Is it not a fact that most of them are entertaining and some of them are even instructive – including the "Jimmy Young Show", on which I appeared this morning?'

Quick as a flash replied Shirley, 'I am sure the Hon. Gentleman appreciates that it was even more instructive when I was on it last month.'

Friday 30 September 1977 marked the tenth anniversary of Radio 2. Naturally, on such occasions our planners and controllers' brains leap into frenzied, one could almost say overheated, action. They plan, scheme, and dream, while we lesser mortals wait with bated breath to discover what is to happen to us. In due course the plans are announced. This time, we

89

were to be despatched to the four corners of the United Kingdom. Not only would we be heard, we would be seen to be heard. The 'JY Prog' was to come from oil rig BP Forties Alpha, 120 miles out in the North Sea, off Aberdeen.

On that Friday morning it looked as though there was no way that could possibly happen. We awoke to find the wind blowing almost a gale. Eventually we were allowed to take off, made our way down the Scottish coast and then headed out to sea. We sighted the BP oil rigs and headed for Forties Alpha. The landing area is painted like an archery target. From the air it looks about the size of a very small pocket handkerchief. As a matter of fact it doesn't look all that big when you are immediately above it. The pilot manoeuvred the helicopter around to the lee side of the rig, and then lost height until we were just *below* the landing platform. I was sitting by him, and he explained that he was still rather worried about the wind, and was getting what shelter he could. He also explained that what he intended to do was to, sort of, pop the helicopter up over the top and plonk it down on the landing area. After what seemed like an eternity he said to me, 'All right then, this is where we find out whether I can fly the bloody thing.' Saying no more, up we went and down we popped.

It was bitterly cold on the rig and we gratefully hurried below. We were handed hot mugs of coffee and, as we began to thaw out, started to remove our heavy outer clothes. At least the others did. As I began to disrobe the gentleman in charge of the rig said, 'Keep yours on, Jim. I thought, to get some background for the broadcast, you'd like to be shown around.'

My guide duly arrived and back out into the arctic conditions we went. Oil rigs may look tiny from the air but, I can assure you they're a helluva size when you're actually standing on one. The wind shrieked and howled. The sea lashed against the giant legs of the rig. It was almost as though all the elements thought we had no right to be there and were doing their best to get rid of us. Standing on one of the outside gantry walks in weather like that is an uncanny, and slightly unnerving, experience. You are out of sight of land, standing on what is rather like a jumbo size Meccano strip of metal, similar to the ones you used to build things with as a kid. As you look through the holes beneath you, you can see the sea lashing away at the very foundations of the rig. You cling on to the guard rail from which the wind is doing its very best to dislodge you, and you are literally surrounded by the North Sea. Just you, on a lump of metal, in the middle of nowhere. I was very glad to get back to the comfort, warmth and security below deck. In fact, after all that, the broadcast itself was easy though predictably, of course, I returned with what Terry Wogan would call 'a nasty touch of the bronichals'.

Ariel, the BBC House magazine, also celebrated the first ten years of Radios 1 and 2. In a full page article headed 'Growth of the JY Politics Show' it said, 'Radios 1 and 2 have come a long way in ten years. But few programmes have developed like the "Jimmy Young Show". Here we look at how the "JY Prog" has changed style, yet remains one of the most popular shows on Radio.'

Regardless of the daily pressures on all of us who work on the programme, the picture which accompanied the article spoke volumes. It says a great deal for the happy working atmosphere we share that many of the names, Harry Walters, John Gurnett, Mike Rhodes, Thelma Blickett, Anne Crane, Suzanne Adams, and Jacquie Lloyd-Ward had not only been with the programme for a long time before the picture was taken, but are still here now. I think we're all hanging on for the end of the first fifty years and the gold watch, but just in case we were tempted to relax a little there came one of those periodic BBC shake ups.

The big news was that Sacha Distel was coming to brighten up Sunday lunchtimes on Radio 2 where, as the *Evening Standard* of 9 November said, 'His silky voice will woo women listeners'. Sacha got the headlines. Lower down in the newspaper articles, among what in theatre-billing days we used to call the 'Wines and Spirits', were details of the accompanying musical chairs. These involved an extra half hour lie-in in bed for Terry Wogan, and moves for Pete Murray, Ray Moore, David Hamilton and myself. The 'JY Prog' was to start ninety minutes earlier, at 10.00 a.m. instead of 11.30 a.m.

Oddly enough it was the time slot I had always wanted since I began the programme back in 1973. I thought the size of our audience was likely to increase, and in due course it did. It put a great deal of extra pressure on us of course, most especially on John Gurnett and Mike Rhodes. My telephone conference with John would still take place at 8 o'clock in the morning. Now, however, instead of having three-and-a-half hours in which to line up speakers on our various topics, John and Mike would have just two hours to prepare for the beginning of the programme. It looked a formidable task, and so it proved. However, they coped, and are still coping, magnificently. But then, as I've always said, they're the best in the business.

The programme has, I am happy to say, always grabbed more than its fair share of headlines. 1978 began as we wanted it to continue with someone important choosing to make a key statement on the 'JY Programme'. Tory leader, Margaret Thatcher, was speaking about immigration and said, 'We shall have better race relations if we don't have these vast numbers coming in, with the prospect of them coming in indefinitely. We cannot go on taking in people at the rate of 40,000 to 50,000 a year. It just can't go on. What most of us want is to live in perfect harmony with the people who are here. And those who are here must have equal rights and responsibilities.' Of the National Front she said, 'I cannot condemn them too strongly.' While, of her critics she said, 'What these people are saying is that we, in politics, cannot discuss the issues that really concern people.'

Fleet Street went to town with headlines like, 'Maggie in attack on "these absurd critics".' 'Race Row – Maggie hits back', 'Callaghan in race attack on Maggie', 'Maggie stands firm'.

This was just the sort of small coup our team revelled in and we were determined to keep our listeners as close as possible to the eye of the storm. And at this particular moment, January 1978, the storm clouds causing most concern were those over the Middle East.

8-Cairo and Jerusalem

Following the success of our 1977 Moscow broadcasts we had been encouraged to mount a similar operation, and as I have indicated the Middle East, as ever in turmoil, seemed the place to go. Accordingly we put forward, as a suggestion, two programmes: one from Cairo, and one from Jerusalem. We were given the go ahead. Producer Harry Walters leaped into action at once. Nobody is better than Harry at writing carefully-worded letters and putting out diplomatic feelers, which he did. The result was that in April 1978 Harry, plus Geoffrey Owen, Head of Radio 2, chief researcher John Gurnett and engineer John Ford set out for the Middle East to 'recce' the two programmes. At a press conference called for 30 May the BBC was able to announce that in Cairo, in addition to discussing matters like the Egyptian economy, rights of women, press freedom and British business interests, I had also been given provisional permission to interview President Sadat. William Davis, writing in the *Daily Express* on 2 June let off a blast on this particular aspect of the visit. In his column he said, 'Stung by criticism of his peace initiative with Israel, which has got nowhere, the thin-skinned Sadat has seized an opposition newspaper, and cracked down on other sections of the Press.' He continued, 'Sixty journalists are under investigation for "defaming their country abroad". Sadat has just agreed to be interviewed on the "Jimmy Young Programme". I hope JY gives him hell.'

Well, certainly the interview was to turn into a bumpy ride for both of us.

Our flight to Egypt was scheduled for Wednesday 7 June, with the broadcast from Cairo taking place on Friday 9 June. The plan then was to fly to Israel over the weekend, and broadcast from Jerusalem on Monday 12 June. The party would consist of our trusty engineers Alan Wilson and John Ford, secretary Liz Sugden, researchers John Gurnett and Mike Rhodes, producer Harry Walters, Controller of Radios 1 and 2 Charles McLelland, and myself.

We were particularly fortunate that the party was being headed by Charles McLelland. True, we already knew that he was a first-rate travelling companion and, when necessary, morale booster. However, on this particular trip he had one asset even more important than these. Prior to his appointment as Controller Radios 1 and 2, he had been Head of the BBC's Arabic Service. As Charles told the *Glasgow Herald* (for which paper he had at one time worked), 'I do know where to lay hands on a few "fixers" in Cairo.'

The trip had something of an eventful beginning. After the 7 June edition of the programme, we piled into cars and headed for Heathrow. We checked in, boarded our British Airways aircraft, and set out for Egypt. All very smooth so far. But not for long. We were about half-way across the English Channel when the Captain made an announcement: 'Nothing to worry about of course, folks, but our radar's packed up. We can't go on without it, so we'll have to go back to London to get it fixed.'

I reckon it's always time to hide under the seat when your captain tells you not to worry. Then he said it a second time. 'Oh, by the way, nothing to worry about of course, but, just to be on the safe side, we're dumping most of our fuel before landing at Heathrow.'

Now, although not particularly brave, I am not one of those passengers known in airline circles as a 'white knuckle job'. Nonetheless, a couple of 'Nothing to worry about folks', plus the sight of all that fuel streaming out of the tanks, certainly brought the colour to my cheeks.

94

Anyway, we crept back to Heathrow without, to my great relief, having to swim for it. Because of this delay we arrived in Cairo very late, very tired, and longing to get to bed. We were driven to the legendary Shepherds Hotel, already dreaming of clean sheets and long, deep, beautiful sleep. What we actually should have been dreaming about was the biggest pile driver in the world. This was at work immediately outside our hotel bedroom windows, and it thudded away relentlessly, every minute of every hour of every day and every night that we were there.

Thursday 8 June was quite a day. President Sadat was staying at his Palace at Ismailia, some sixty miles from Cairo. There was still no cast iron agreement that I would be allowed to interview him. However, we had been told that, if we cared to present ourselves at the Palace at 10.30 a.m. on Thursday morning, it was just possible that we would be allowed to record an interview for transmission the following day. Accordingly we set off from Cairo and arrived outside the Palace at Ismailia in good time, just before 10.30. Already waiting outside the Palace was a television outside broadcast van. We parked next to it. Included in our party was one of the 'fixers' to whom Charles McLelland had made reference earlier. Her name was Sana-el-Saed. She walked across the road to the guard on the gate leading into the Palace grounds. It should have been a short conversation. Something on the lines of, 'Will you please telephone the Palace and let the President know we are here?' It was *not* a short conversation. As a matter of fact it was an extremely *long* conversation with much waving of arms. It also, towards the end, got quite heated. Sana came back across the road towards us. She was flushed, and very angry. 'They say the President is giving no interviews at all today', she reported.

'I could have told you that,' said a voice conversationally, 'we've been waiting here for two hours. We're just leaving.'

It was one of the crew from the television van parked next to us. With a cheery wave, almost a sailor's farewell, they left. By this time it was past 11 o'clock, and midday in June in Egypt can be, if you'll pardon the expression, 'hotter'n Hell'. We groaned and collapsed on the ground, each sitting in our individual pool of sweat. But Sana was about to prove herself a little gem. As she spoke I realized why she had looked flushed and angry. As far as she was concerned she had fixed for me to interview President Sadat, and her professional pride was at stake. Very firmly, and her voice had a steely, cutting edge, she said, 'Stay exactly where you are. Do not move until I get back.' She then jumped into her motor car and disappeared up the road in a huge cloud of Egyptian dust. Down the middle of the road outside the Palace at Ismailia runs a grassy bank. Palm trees grow up from it at regular intervals, providing some kind of shelter from the blazing midday sun. We gratefully threw ourselves down in whatever shade we could find to await Sana's return, whenever that might be.

It was 2 p.m., and we had almost given up hope when, in the distance, we saw the dust cloud that heralds all movement. Sana skidded to a halt and jumped out of her car. 'Quick,' she said, 'into Ismailia town for some lunch, then we come back and do the interview.' We gratefully piled into our van and headed for town. We entered the restaurant and ordered lunch. We were starving. After an age it arrived. It had just been put on the table when the phone rang. Sana answered it. 'Right, that's it', she said; 'we leave now.' We never did have lunch.

Back to the Palace, and this time we actually got through the gate. Secretly I was still thinking; I'll believe it when I'm actually doing it. We were shown into a guard room and left there. All except Sana. She was taken on into the Palace itself, which at least seemed to be a hopeful sign. Eventually she came running back. 'Now,' she said, 'quickly, we have thirty minutes.' We were escorted towards the Palace, but not into it. Instead we walked around the main building and on to the Palace lawn. As we rounded the corner we walked into the most breathtakingly beautiful scene. The lawn is rich and green. It runs right down to the Suez Canal. Trees, and a profusion of richly coloured flowers, shrubs and bushes make an immediate and powerful visual impact. In the background huge ships, ploughing their way through the Suez Canal, complete the picture. Seated close to the water's edge was President Sadat. Standing next to him, and in earnest conversation with him, was Sana. You see what I mean by a gem. She had fought, and won, on our behalf.

It was now 4 p.m. and after all that time in the sun, we were totally exhausted. For me, however, the day was only just about to begin. I told myself, a pro never cares how tired he feels, all he cares about is whether he gives a good performance. The next thirty minutes would show. There was a very stiff breeze blowing and technical expert Alan Wilson speedily made his wishes known to me. 'We've got to get him inside, Jim', said Alan; 'we shall never record him successfully out here.' I beckoned Sana over and explained the situation. Sana spoke to the President. I don't speak Egyptian of course, but I didn't need to. The look on his face and the tone of his voice told me all I needed to know. There was no way the President was going inside. 'You do it here,' said he, 'or you don't do it at all.'

There was a hedge about thirty feet from where the President was sitting. 'Well, let's see if we can get him behind that, Jim,' said Alan, 'at least that might give us a little bit of shelter from the wind.'

I whispered to Sana. Sana whispered to the President. Yes, reluctantly, he would move that far. We moved, and tried again. 'Still no good,' said Alan, 'we must get him inside the Palace.'

I said, 'Alan, if you think there's any way I'm going to get the President of Egypt to move twice in one day, against his will, you've got another think coming. We stay here.' By this time we had lost over ten of our precious thirty minutes. We began. I had divided the interview, roughly, into two parts. The first half was about general Middle East problems, with special reference, of course, to Egypt and Israel. The second half was to deal with Sadat's problems at home.

The first part of the interview went relatively smoothly. The President made the expected references to being disappointed by Israel's reaction to his Jerusalem initiative. He confessed to being 'stunned' by Israel's proposals to retain its settlements in the Sinai desert under Israeli army protection. He stated flatly that Israel had no alternative other than to withdraw to pre-1967 borders.

I asked President Sadat about attacks on his Government from within Egypt and I went on to ask him about the referendum he had recently held to decide what measures should be taken against the most vocal of his critics. How did this square with his statement that he had created for Egypt a liberalized parliamentary system?

According to the *Guardian* newspaper's report of this part of the interview, 'President Sadat, his voice rising in volume replied, "I was very furious with your Radio when you took their part in the doubt campaign." He continued, "I told them, either convey to British public opinion the real picture, or not at all. I'm only asking for the truth and nothing but the truth." '

Certainly the *Guardian* was accurate that the President's voice rose, and continued to rise. What they couldn't know, of course, was that he was leaning forward around the microphone and shaking his forefinger at me. I pressed the President further on the allegations that he was suppressing criticism. His voice became even louder. He continued to be very agitated and angry. And then, quite suddenly, the most extraordinary thing happened. He broke off in mid-sentence, returned to being the charming, charismatic man he really was and said, 'I must apologize, my friend, if I was sharp. I know I was, and I am sorry. But I must explain that Thursday is my fast day, and I have not eaten or drunk anything since last night. Even worse than that, on fast day I cannot even smoke my pipe, and *that* makes me *very* irritable.'

It also, I thought, made that great man very human. His murder three years later deprived the world of a sane, clear-sighted statesman who will be sorely missed.

Over the weekend we flew to Israel where we were due to broadcast from Jerusalem on Monday 12 June.

Put like that, it sounds fairly simple. However, at that time relations between Egypt and Israel were so strained that it was anything but simple. One was not allowed to fly direct. Indeed it was necessary for there to be seen to be a complete break. Accordingly, having worked our way through three sets of security checks at Cairo airport we flew Egyptian airlines to Athens. This was a particularly tiresome and irritating journey.

Not so much because it was all that far, but because we were conscious that we were heading, roughly speaking, in the opposite direction to that in which we wanted to travel. Eventually we arrived at Athens where, just to put a little icing on the cake, we lost our luggage! Having finally retrieved it, all that remained was to negotiate the second leg. TWA to Ben Gurion. It's odd how often it's the little things in life that stick in the mind. One such happening occurred as we came in to land at Ben Gurion Airport. The aircraft was crowded with American Jews, taking a holiday, and at the same time making a pilgrimage, to Israel. As we landed they all applauded. A great many of them wept. It was a first-hand demonstration of the depth of feeling of the Jewish people for Israel. Even to a non Jew it was an extremely moving moment. As we were driven from the airport to Jerusalem we noticed the ruins of burned-out lorries which, for some reason, seemed to have been preserved. When we enquired we were told that indeed they were burned-out lorries. They had been destroyed during the war and were now retained as war memorials. The Russians last year with their tank trap, and now the Israelis with their lorries. I wondered why people had such a morbid fascination with war.

Eventually we arrived at our hotel, the Jerusalem Plaza. It is modern, chrome and glass. Sleek, sophisticated, and Americanized, it has none of the history or ambience of Shepherds in Cairo. On the other hand, nor did it have a pile driver, I was pleased to note. One thing it did have though. A simply marvellous view. From our balconies we could see clearly across Jerusalem, to the Old City and the Mount of Olives. We all hoped that we might have time to see at least a little of The Holy City. Little did we know, we were going to have almost a whole day to spare.

Things seldom go as planned in the broadcasting business, and this trip was to be no exception. One of the most important areas to cover while in Israel was President Sadat's courageous peace initiative. It had been arranged for me to talk to Israel's Deputy Prime Minister, Professor Yigael Yadin, about it. However, during the course of our flight from Egypt to Israel, the Israeli Cabinet had called a crucial meeting, which meant that

Professor Yadin would not be available for the broadcast. What happened next was described by producer, Harry Walters, as demonstrating the flexibility of both the 'Jimmy Young Programme' and Radio 2. It also demonstrated the good luck of having Controller Radios 1 and 2 with us because Charles McLelland, on the spot, quite simply took the decision to postpone the broadcast for one whole day and transmit on 13 June instead. For once in our lives this meant that we actually had the luxury of a whole day in which to do some sightseeing.

I find it difficult to sum up what I felt about Jerusalem. True, we visited all the legendary places, and I was glad that I had seen them, and would never forget doing so. But somehow, for me, the Bible didn't come alive. Perhaps I expected too much. Perhaps I was too put off by what seemed blatant, and at times, extreme, commercialism. The only other thing of interest that happened that day was that I broke a rib. I managed to fall down a flight of stairs at the hotel. And should you be thinking what I think you're thinking, I wasn't. I was rushed off to the doctor who strapped up my ribs tighter than anyone had done since my rugby playing days, and I realized then that my Jerusalem broadcasts were going to be conducted in the classic bent-over-holding-my-side-does-it-hurt-only-when-I-breathe-style.

On the morning of Tuesday 13 June we had a recording to do. For a programme which, as I said at the beginning of this book, prides itself on always going out live we seemed to be doing a lot of pre-recording. The fact was, though, that although the Deputy Prime Minister was most happy to be interviewed, he could not be with us for the actual transmission. So, once again, it was pre-record or nothing. Mike Rhodes, Harry, John Gurnett, Alan Wilson and I presented ourselves on Tuesday morning at a very ordinary looking house, situated not too far from our Jerusalem hotel. We were shown up to the first floor and into a rather dark, very quiet room, where we were joined by Deputy Prime Minister Yadin. I put it to Professor Yadin that President Sadat had given his peace initiative a further two months to succeed, and that he had accused the Israeli Government of being intransigent. Said the Deputy Prime Minister, 'I think it is naïve of President

Sadat to think that one can solve a very deep conflict of many many years within two months, like an instant coffee solution.' He went on, 'President Sadat, whom I think is a great man, and whose courage I admire, is making a mistake by setting these dates.'

I said, 'But the whole Israeli Parliament applauded him when he spoke there on his peace initiative.'

Said Professor Yadin, 'The Parliament only applauded him because he said what he said in Jerusalem and not somewhere else. But they still disagree with him.'

It seemed that President Sadat had presented the Israelis with what he saw as his conditions. The Israelis had, mistakenly, interpreted them as Sadat's opening offer, and subject to negotiation. Since then, it appeared, no dialogue had taken place between them. I said that I found this terribly depressing, even frightening. I was even more depressed when I heard Professor Yadin's reply, 'I regret that, it appears, the only way I can talk to President Sadat is "through" Jimmy Young. If only I could talk to him direct I am sure we could find a solution.' It hadn't taken very long to see why Middle East negotiations wore out good men very quickly. On behalf of all of us I thanked Deputy Prime Minister Yadin for granting us the interview, and we emerged from the dark, quiet room into the already burning hot sunshine of a Jerusalem morning.

One of the most fascinating moments in the broadcast which followed later that day was when I found myself interviewing an Arab Israeli. This may seem like a contradiction in terms but, of course, it isn't. In 1978, when we were in Israel, there were in fact 1.7 million Arabs living under Israeli control, and talking to me was one of them, Zaiden Atashi. I asked him what was the relationship between the Israeli Jews and the minorities. He bridled instantly. He said, 'To start with I don't like to use the term minority. I am Israeli and I am equal. All the Israeli Arabs who stayed after the Independence War have been granted Israeli status and equal rights.' The farther we went the more complicated it became. There were Arab Arabs and Israeli Israelis. There were also Arab Israelis, almost more proudly Israeli than the Israeli Jews themselves. I asked him if the Arabs inside Israel looked to the P.L.O. for leadership.

He said that, in his opinion unfortunately, in recent years some Arab individuals, mainly of the younger generation, had been claiming the right to Palestinian determination, a phenomenon which had not existed before. 'But,' he said, 'we are a democratic society, so everyone has the right to say whatever he wants.'

I asked Zaiden whether he accepted the accusations that the Israeli Government was, 'intransigent'. I was confronted with the unusual situation of an Arab, not only denying that the Israeli Government was intransigent, but going on to say, 'What about the intransigence of our neighbouring States, Syria, Jordan, Algeria, South Yemen and Libya, what about *their* intransigence. They do not want even the existence of the State of Israel in the Middle East. Why do you always ask this question of the Israelis?' Zaiden raised one other interesting point. I had mentioned that the Arab birth rate in Israel was higher than the Jewish birth rate. He agreed that it was in fact much higher, and went further to say that, within ten years, he could see there being at least as many, and quite possibly more, Arabs in Israel than there were Jews. I asked him what he thought would be the political implications of that.

The staunch Israeli surfaced immediately. He said, 'I do not want to see the Israeli Knesset [Parliament] represented by fifty per cent Jews and fifty per cent Arabs, that would create more problems than it would solve. We are moderate Arabs and I do not want it to come to an unfortunate civil war. I want to keep the State of Israel as it was envisaged by the Jewish Zionist leaders.'

I talked to economist and political analyst, Dan Bavly, about Israel's internal problems. It sounded remarkably like doing an interview about Britain's economy a year in advance. The Israeli Government was trying to move towards encouraging free enterprise. The liberalization of foreign currency controls, tackling a high inflation rate caused, the Government said, by Government overspending and the trade unions trying to get big wage increases to keep up with inflation. Shades of British things to come!

I talked about the rights and freedoms of Israeli women to Ora Namir, a Labour member of the Knesset, and former

Chairwoman of the State Commission on the Status of Women. In a country in which women, by law, are equal, and which had, in Golda Meir, one of the first women Prime Ministers, I fully expected to hear that women played a very full and active role in all areas. Not so. I asked about the role of Israeli women in the armed forces. Ora replied, 'We are not pleased with the status of women in the Army. Women can contribute much more than they do today. Women are less and less involved in most fields of work in the Army, and are not used in combat.' I knew Ora had recommended that women in the forces should be allowed to train as pilots, and I asked her about it. 'Nothing came of that,' she said, 'the Ministry of Defence refused to accept it.' We talked of housing and education but, in spite of equality by law, a few facts emerged very clearly. There were fewer women in the Knesset than ever before, fewer women showed an active interest in politics, and Israeli women were, more than ever, wrapped up in their families. I asked Ora why she thought this was. She said, 'There is hardly a family in Israel which didn't lose a son, a husband, or a relative in one of the wars.' She went on, 'At times like these, women want to devote more and more of their time to their family.' The day had its surprises; first the possibility of there being, in just ten years, more Arabs than Jews in the Jewish National State and now the nation's women, many trained by the armed forces, feeling the urge to return to the role of homemaker and earth mother.

Once again our time was up and we had to begin our journey home. As with our Moscow trip we had arranged a 'balancing programme' for the following Thursday, 15 June. This, as I have explained earlier in the book, was so that, if it was thought there had been any serious imbalance in our broadcasts abroad, there would be an opportunity to correct it. As it happened there was no imbalance, but the Thursday programme went ahead anyway. It produced a bizarre happening, rather frightening at the time, but, viewed retrospectively, very funny both for the victim, and all of us on the team. I was to interview Greville Janner, and Christopher Mayhew, well known for their expert knowledge of the Jews and Arabs respectively.

103

The programme turned out to be quite lively. An article in *The Listener* of 22 June said, 'The follow up discussion between Christopher Mayhew and Greville Janner M.P. turned into quite a humdinger when Jimmy failed to detach the two experts from each other's throats.'

The most painful moment, however, had nothing to do with broadcasting, except in as much as it demonstrated the one hundred per cent professionalism of the gentleman concerned. Christopher Mayhew had a bad back. Indeed it was so bad that he sometimes wore a surgical corset. On this occasion, for whatever the reason, he wasn't wearing it. The broadcast was going beautifully and Christopher and Greville, both in great form, were making their points strongly. Suddenly, in mid-sentence, Christopher twisted sideways to make a point. He stifled a yell, grabbed his back, fell to the floor, and couldn't move. However, and how about this for quick thinking, with his other hand he pulled the microphone down the two feet or so to where his mouth now was, and continued with his answer. As soon as he had finished the sentence I closed the microphone. In rushed the studio staff, plus John, Mike and Harry, and then the pantomime began. Could we move Christopher? We could not! There he was, on the floor unable to get up, or move at all for that matter. He told us, 'Please get a cab to rush home and pick up my surgical corset.' Meanwhile, our pressing problem was what to do with our next guest, due in my studio at any moment. We could hardly step over Christopher. Five minutes of pondering brought us to the conclusion that our only option was to move him exactly as he was, and that, eventually, is what we did. Poor Christopher. We managed to get him into the control room next door, and there he lay, in agony, until medical help and surgical corset arrived as hot foot as we were able to manage it.

We've all had several good laughs about it since, but my lasting admiration has always been for the tremendous professionalism of a man who, even while in agony, had the presence of mind to adjust the microphone and keep right on broadcasting.

9- Confrontation

After the excitement and demands of a difficult broadcast far away from home base, one is always a little worried in case a return to the rather more mundane world of daily broadcasting may produce a lack of excitement, even a complete let down in the amount of adrenalin flowing. That was certainly not going to be the case on this occasion.

Thursday 6 July 1978 saw the return to my studio of Edward Heath. He was coming in to talk to me on the subject of youth and unemployment. This booking had been made some two weeks previously and, while interesting, was expected to be fairly low key. However, as it happened, Ted had made a speech on the previous evening at Stocksbridge, South Yorkshire, in the Penistone by-election campaign, during the course of which he had said that he would fight alongside Mrs Thatcher 'just as hard as I have ever done'. This, to all of us on the programme, sounded like conciliatory moves from Mr Heath in the direction of Mrs Thatcher. Accordingly, we decided to lead into the interview with his comments on the speech. In the event it was not to be quite that easy. Ted came into the studio and asked me what I was going to lead in with. I told him of the revised plan. His eyes went steely, as they do when he is angry, 'I don't wish to talk about the speech', he said.

'But it's the big news in all the papers today', I said.

'Exactly,' said Ted, 'so we're not going to get any more out of it.' Swiftly I decided that I wasn't going to get anywhere like that. I therefore switched the whole interview back again, and led in with the problems of young people facing unemployment. For the next ten minutes, as we talked, I was trying to do four things at once. I was asking questions, listening to answers, commenting on those answers, and also trying to decide whether or not I had the guts to confront a former Prime Minister, by bringing up a subject which I knew he didn't want to discuss. Eventually I came to the conclusion that I was on to a loser either way, but a bigger loser if I didn't than if I did. When a break came in the conversation I took a deep breath. I said, 'I know that before we began talking I asked whether you would talk about last night's speech. I also realize that you said under no circumstances would you do so, but you see the point is, if I *don't* ask you about it I shall get shot by my eight million listeners.'

'True,' said Mr Heath, 'and if you *do* ask me you may well get shot by me.'

I said the only thing which came into my mind, knowing that the interview was 'live', 'Well, I'll start from the basis that the worst thing that can happen is that you walk out on me.' He didn't, of course. He's far too professional for tantrums like that. He gave me a further first-rate fifteen minutes.

As the final question, I asked him, 'Would you accept the offer of a post in the Cabinet if the Conservatives won?'

With a wry smile he said, 'I think we'd better concentrate on winning the election first don't you?'

Producer Harry Walters was later walking him to the front door of Broadcasting House. Seeking to smooth any ruffled feathers, although of course there weren't any, Harry said, 'I hope Jim didn't upset you too much, Mr Heath.'

Said Mr Heath, this time with a broad grin and the heave of the shoulders, 'Oh, I knew he'd get me in the end, Harry.'

I was born in a little town in Gloucestershire called Cinderford, and my mother lived there all her life. Indeed a relative of mine, Ken Wakefield, is still in business there as a barber. I was about to be asked to return to my roots.

Cinderford was going to get its first ever Mayor, and I was

asked if I would be willing to go back home to invest him with the title and regalia. With the greatest of pleasure I agreed; and, on 5 August 1978, in the crowded town centre of Cinderford, I installed Councillor Frank Beard as Cinderford's first Mayor. In return, the Mayor presented me with a scroll, plus the symbolic gold key to Cinderford. I have it at home alongside the admittance to the Freedom of the City of London granted to me in 1969.

I reflected that, if my dear Mum had still been alive, she, like me, would have been equally proud of both.

The programme produced another 'first' in the autumn of 1978. We commissioned the first National Opinion Poll report ever produced especially for the 'Jimmy Young Programme'. It was called, 'The Young Report' for two reasons. First, because it concerned the attitudes of young people. Second, because it carried the name of the programme which had commissioned it. The results surprised many people, especially those expecting revolutionary ideals.

Said the *Daily Mirror* on 26 September, 'Kids today are a jolly good bunch. They favour the trad values that Mum and Dad cherish. As for being more liberal and way out – forget it.'

On the same day the *Daily Express*, in its leading article, said, 'Youth is conservative – with a small "c". A public opinion poll conducted for the "Jimmy Young Show" reveals overwhelming support among the 15–21 age group for law and order (including the return of hanging). They also favour fair treatment for minorities, and the institution of marriage: in short, stability, tranquility, authority – and toleration. Which must make some of our middle-aged trendies, still dreaming of their fun revolution of the Sixties, wonder what has happened.'

In fact ninety per cent of young people surveyed wanted tougher punishment for vandals, and sixty-four per cent supported capital punishment for all murderers. Most were against the legalizing of cannabis, and most believed that, if teenagers wanted to take drugs, older people should try to stop them. A majority agreed that 'homosexuals should be treated like everybody else' and a similar proportion disagreed with a suggestion that coloured immigrants should be sent home.

All very normal and stable. Even to the last finding which was that the family are tops, and their heroes are Mum and Dad. However, the one outstanding niggle of the young was highlighted by 'The Young Report'.

Concluded the report, 'twenty-four per cent thought life had become more difficult. Many of them blamed the job situation for this.'

'Unemployment is by far the most serious political issue as far as young people are concerned.'

A forewarning of things to come.

You may remember that January 1979 saw the country enjoying, if that's the word I want, just about the worst of all worlds. We were approaching the middle of the 'Winter of Discontent', and everybody seemed to be in a dispute of some kind. The secondary picketing disputes were becoming extremely ugly, and there were reports of panic buying of food. To cap it all, we shivered in the grip of the Big Freeze. The pickets, and every so often the fists, flew. And when questioned as to where some of the flying pickets were coming from, a shop steward was quoted as saying, 'I don't care if the pickets come from bloody Bertram Mills Circus.'

The big interview of the 'Winter of Discontent' came on 31 January. Once again I talked to Conservative Leader, Mrs Margaret Thatcher. We spoke about a pay freeze and she said, 'I would support one if things got very bad.'

We discussed wage bargaining and the balance of power as between unions and Government. We talked about the closed shop, picketing, and the introduction of secret ballots. She said, 'It's no earthly use saying anything for a quiet life. I certainly don't regard what we have now as a quiet life.'

In a reference to the fact that there were 220 bodies stored in a Merseyside warehouse which couldn't be buried because of a strike by gravediggers she said, 'Why, you can't even get a decent burial.'

I still felt, however, that the quote which would encapsulate her whole feeling about the situation had somehow eluded me. I decided to persist. I asked her how she would feel if, in the event that she became Prime Minister, unions refused to co-operate with her. Even perhaps went so far as actually to confront her. It had taken a long time, but when she spoke I knew I was listening to the paragraph which described exactly how she felt, and what she was determined to do about it. She said, 'If someone is confronting our essential liberties and inflicting injury and hardship on the sick, the elderly, and children then I will confront them. By God I will confront them.'

So, that was the gut feeling of Margaret Thatcher about the 'Winter of Discontent'. Whether it would endear her to, or alienate her from, eight million listeners remained to be seen.

A bright spot in a dark world was that Mike Smith, our doctor, discovered Joggers' Nipple.

Said reporter Michael O'Flaherty in the *Daily Express* in Manchester on 7 February 1979, 'A hazard was revealed yesterday on the "Jimmy Young Show" by Dr Mike Smith, who said, "Doctors' waiting rooms are becoming more and more full of patients complaining of sore nipples. More often than not they are joggers. It is becoming a well-known phenomenon. It's caused by friction between the nipple and the track-suit or vest. We call it "Joggers' Nipple".' I don't know whether it is a well-known phenomenon or not, but I figured that, just at that moment, anything that raised a flicker of a smile *had* to be a good thing. Much has been spoken and written about the ability of us Brits to keep our sense of humour when all around us is crumbling. Certainly it's true of the folk who listen to the 'JY Prog'.

Early in April I was interviewing the Business Editor of the *Guardian* about a report which suggested that British Leyland were thinking of entering into a partnership with a Japanese car firm. Quick as a flash our telephones began to ring. Said one listener, 'I think it's a plot to get all the Japanese firms linked with British firms, then we can kill 'em off one by one.' The comment of a British Leyland Union official was even more succinct. Said he, 'Absence makes the plant grow Honda.' Boom Boom.

The General Election was scheduled for 3 May 1979 and we

mounted special programmes with the leaders of each of the three main political parties, David Steel, Margaret Thatcher and James Callaghan. We had, on several occasions, asked whether Mr Callaghan would appear on the programme, but this was the first time he had agreed to do so. Not unnaturally, I wondered how it would be. In the event, we got on like a house on fire. He answered every question, covered all the ground I had hoped to cover, and the interview received big press coverage, including a quote which even the team was certain I would never get: in answer to a question about his relations with the far left, Big Jim said, 'No one's going to push *me* around.' As a famous lady once said, 'Well, he would say that, wouldn't he?'

Our 'Election Special' programme ran from 10 a.m. to midday. Then it was away for a couple of hours rest, returning at 9 p.m. for an 11 p.m. kick-off. In Studio 4A with me were the ever faithful Brian Curtois, plus Adam Raphael of *The Observer*, Bill Davis and Clive Jenkins. Once again I struck lucky. It was a particularly well-chosen team: Brian Curtois, studious, quiet and well informed; Adam Raphael, extrovert and knowledgeable; Bill and Clive, of course, were just made for each other. Both are marvellous characters, masters of the vocal rapier thrust. Both possess a wonderfully funny and, when necessary, acid wit. And, short of Death striking them a mortal blow, neither is ever likely to be stuck for a word or two. To be honest, with a team like that, I didn't need to do very much. As the results poured in, it speedily became obvious that Britain was about to have its first woman Prime Minister.

We worked until 3.45 a.m. Then it was a few hours' sleep and back to start again at 10 a.m. on the morning of Friday, 4 May. It was hell on wheels of course. But wonderfully exciting. I wouldn't have missed it for anything. I tried to keep a list of the people I interviewed. But after David Howell, Merlyn Rees, Jim Prior, David Alton, Ian Mikardo, John Silkin, Hugh Rossi, The Chairman of the Stock Exchange, Norman St John-Stevas (you won't be able to call her The Blessed Margaret any more, Norman!), Bill Rodgers, Sir Geoffrey Howe, David Steel, Tom Jackson, Peregrine Worsthorne and Peter Shore, I decided to pack it in. We finally finished at 2.30 p.m. on Friday afternoon and, one way and another, reckoned it had gone fairly well.

We decided to stagger off home to bed and I climbed into my car and set off. I was half-way down George Street, London W1 when it happened. I was stationary in the middle of the road, my indicator winking away, waiting to turn right, quietly happy, relaxed and reflecting on a job, seemingly well done. There was a crash and I was thrown forward against the wind- screen. Even in the split second it took my head to travel from head rest to windscreen I remember thinking, 'Oh Gawd, not again.' It had happened to me before, back in 1970, you see. Once again, a gentleman had driven into the back of my sta- tionary car. I got out, bruised but in one piece, and we ex- changed names and addresses. He begged me not to notify my insurance company, and said he would prefer to settle privately. You will have guessed the rest of course. It was a false name and address. We never did trace him. It cost me £297 in repair bills. Had I had any sense I would have written to the legal beagle on the 'JY Prog' about it.

As I have mentioned before, one of the nice things I've dis- covered since I've been interviewing 'heavyweights' is that the really able people usually have an excellent sense of humour. This was about to be demonstrated again. Joel Barnett had been Chief Secretary to the Treasury, under the previous La- bour Government. A man of extremely high intelligence, he doesn't let this weigh heavily upon him. On the contrary, he is always laughing and joking; a friendly, very pleasant man to be with. I was interviewing him on 21 May 1979 with regard to the Tory Budget, due on 12 June. Joel went through the usual ritual shadow boxing, of course. State of the economy not our fault, no skeletons in the cupboard, horrible times ahead under this wicked Tory Government. All par for the course and to be expected. However, it was when we turned to inflation that Joel had me, and all of us in the studio, falling about. I asked Joel how, in terms that everyone could under- stand, he would define inflation.

'Well,' said Joel, 'it's rather like the lady who asked her husband the very same question. Her husband said, "Well dear, you remember when we were first married you were twenty years of age, and your measurements were 36–24–36. Now you're fifty years of age and your measurements are 42–42–42. In other words, there's more of you, but you're not worth as much." That's inflation.'

It's very refreshing to meet someone who, even when trying to balance the nation's books, and that can't be easy, manages to retain his sense of humour.

I had a holiday fixed for June and, after the election coverage, I must say that I was really looking forward to it. We suddenly realized that the Chancellor had, rather inconsiderately, plonked his Budget down smack in the middle of it. Problems.

The Beeb made the decision that they would do a mini coverage of the Budget without me. They then changed their mind and decided upon what many people would probably have thought of as a lumber, but what I regarded as the greatest compliment they could have paid me: they asked me whether I would be willing to fly back from my holiday on 13 June, to do two special programmes. One with the Shadow Chancellor of the Exchequer, Denis Healey, on the 14th, and one with the new Chancellor, Sir Geoffrey Howe, on the 15th. I gladly agreed, did the two programmes, and then flew back to continue my holiday.

By the time I returned from holiday the news of my impending O.B.E. had leaked out. It's hard to tell you how kind people were. Letters flooded in from listeners, trade union leaders, politicians, and colleagues in the business. It was an honour I was most pleased to receive, not just for myself, but for the whole team associated with the programme, who had worked so hard to make it into the success it had become.

ABOVE: All set for a BBC Radio first. As soon as the morning programme was over, we flew to Moscow.
BELOW: Jak's interpretation of my Moscow trip

'You think this is torture, you should hear some of my programmes!'

OPPOSITE: In front of St Basil's Cathedral in Red Square after a broadcasting first.
ABOVE: Celebrating Radio 2's tenth anniversary from BP Forties Alpha.
BELOW: The photo of the JY team taken on 5 October 1977. From left to right: Thelma Blickett, Anne Crane, Liz Sugden, John Gurnett, JY, Harry Walters, Jacquie Lloyd-Ward, Mike Rhodes, Eleanor Marshal, Denis O'Keefe, Suzanne Adams

ABOVE: After my interview with President Sadat in June 1978. From left ro right: Harry Walters, Sana-el-Saed, John Gurnett, President Sadat, Alan Wilson, JY, Charles McLelland

BELOW: BBC Radio and Television's general election team in April 1979. From left to right: Frank Bough, Donald McCormick, John Timpson, David Dimbleby, Robert McKenzie, Brian Redhead, Libby Purves, Robin Day and JY

OPPOSITE: Chancellor of the Exchequer, Sir Geoffrey Howe taking a break from the world of finance to have a spin on the turntable.

OPPOSITE: In top hat and tails, leaving the Palace with my O.B.E.
ABOVE: Co-winners of R.A.D.A.R.'s 'Men of the Year' award; Sebastian Coe, JY and J. P. R. Williams
BELOW LEFT: Mounting the campaign with Dave Lee Travis to help the Manpower Services Commission.
BELOW RIGHT: Cartoon by David Langdon

'I sometimes think a lot of the work of the House could be done equally well on the Jimmy Young Show.'

OPPOSITE: Alicia and I on our return from Florida
ABOVE: Recording songs with musical director, Neil Richardson.
BELOW: Interviewing Labour Leader, James Callaghan.

OPPOSITE: Joan Shenton and I with the 'Thon', Telethon's mascot
RIGHT: With Joan Shenton and Rolf Harris holding up the telephone numbers for people to ring with pledges.
BELOW: In party mood with Terry Wogan and Sheila Tracey

MIDLANDS (BBC Radio Derby: page 72)
3-9 October 1981   Price 20p

BBC Radio
NEW SEASON

RadioTimes

'Over to you, Jimbo'

**Clock in with
Terry Wogan at 7.30 am and
Jimmy Young at 10.0 am,
each weekday on Radio 2.
Inside: clash of the Titans**

ABOVE: Front cover of *Radio Times*
OPPOSITE: A lesson in signing my name in Japanese, ready for our visit to Tokyo

OPPOSITE ABOVE: Terry and I indulging in our morning banter.
OPPOSITE BELOW: The Leader of the Opposition, Michael Foot, warning the 'infantile left that they would be dealt with'.
ABOVE: The Prime Minister returns to the programme.

A view of Terry's studio from the control room

10-Zimbabwe

Our overseas broadcasts in 1977 and 1978, had gone down so well with our listeners that we were once again under pressure to come up with another suitable idea.

Incidentally, lest you should think that these overseas trips are some kind of holiday dreamed up by the BBC to reward us for being good boys and girls, let me speedily disabuse you. It's true that we all look forward to the challenge of actually doing them. Not so rewarding, however, are the weeks of heavy slog researching them, the sheer physical strain of getting to the venues and back, plus the mental strain of actually doing the programmes.

Our project for 1979 was particularly daunting. Rhodesia had been, and still was, much in the news, particularly now, because things seemed to be moving towards a climax. We therefore decided to broadcast from there on 9 and 10 August.

Because of the vast distance involved there was no rush of volunteers from the research department to undertake the 'recce' trip to set things up. However, being the brave man that he is, John Gurnett offered to go, and that was when we discovered the first fly in the ointment. Because of the political situation existing at the time we wouldn't be able to fly direct to Rhodesia. John discovered we would have to fly to Johannesburg first, and then retrace our steps from Johannesburg to Salisbury. Thirteen hours flying to Johannesburg, a further two to Salisbury, fifteen in all. Off set the intrepid

John, to return in due course with a cast list which, to say the least, was impressive. Among others who had agreed to come on the programme and talk to me were a former official of Joshua Nkomo's ZAPU Party; General Walls, the Commander of the Security Forces; the Foreign Minister; and the Prime Minister himself, Bishop Abel Muzorewa.

Our exhausting schedule began on Monday 6 August. We flew the thirteen-hour overnight trip to Johannesburg, rested for three hours in a Jo'Burg hotel, and then embarked for the last, two-hour leg to Salisbury on Tuesday afternoon. The 707 was absolutely packed. It was very hot, and it looked like being a most uncomfortable two hours. However, apart from the smell of bodies, there was also the smell of a great deal of nervous tension in the air. It was to be about one hour and forty minutes before I discovered why.

There was a great deal of bantering from some of the Brits aboard who knew who I was. 'Is your insurance paid up, Jim?' was one remark. 'What are you doing over here, then, Jim, don't you know there's a war on?' was another. Certainly we knew there was a war on. After all we had known that when we'd volunteered to do the broadcast, hadn't we? However, the back chat and ribaldry in the cabin had those few extra decibels in the noise level that come when people are doing a bit of whistling in the dark. And indeed, I suddenly remembered, an Air Rhodesia plane flying between Jo'Burg and Salisbury had been shot down by a ground to air missile not at all that long ago, hadn't it! Anyway, there we were, sealed in, and there wasn't an awful lot we could do about it. What slightly brought the pains on, however, was the announcement when we were about twenty minutes' flying time from Salisbury. The voice said, 'This is your Captain speaking, and this is just to warn you that we are about to make what we call "A security approach".'

Oh, that's interesting, I thought, what's a security approach? Well, a security approach consists of the stewardess pulling down all those little blinds on the windows at the side of the cabin and then, just to be on the safe side, turning out all the lights as well. Quite suddenly we were sitting in what, at that moment, seemed very much like a cramped, flying, blacked-out potential coffin. The war was immediately incredibly real, and very, very close. There was a loud, angry cry from one of the air hostesses. The gentleman sitting behind me had lifted up his blind to try and see where we were. The stewardess raced down the gangway and I quite thought she was going to punch him. Instead she contented herself with swearing at him and snatching the blind down again. I began to think that I'd be glad to get my feet on the ground, and reflected that there wasn't even anything in my contract about the Beeb paying me danger money!

Our traditional luck with the timing of important programmes had worked again. However, it had thrown up, so to speak, the good news and the bad news. The good news was that a very important Commonwealth conference, to be attended by Britain's new Prime Minister, Mrs Thatcher, had been arranged to take place in Lusaka during the week immediately prior to our programmes. This would make them even more topical than ever. The bad news was that the very topicality of Lusaka, and the discussions and decisions being taken there, would render out of date a lot of the research over which we had sweated so long at home. It was obvious that we would have to begin re-researching the first of the two programmes the following morning. I had a funny feeling that all I was going to see of Zimbabwe was my hotel room and the broadcasting studio, and that is exactly how it turned out. For all of us.

Wednesday 8 August dawned hot and clear with none of the heavy humidity which had characterized Johannesburg. It was the sort of day which made me reflect that it would be quite nice to enjoy a bit of sunshine. I already knew, however, that I was destined to go back to London as pale as the day I left. The free copy of the *Salisbury Herald*, thrust under my hotel room door, informed me on the front page that, back in London, the BBC was being picketed.

The 'Campaign Against Racism in the Media' had announced its intention of demonstrating outside Broadcasting House against 'The Young Programmes'. The BBC, however, said that it would ignore the protests, and would go ahead with the programmes as planned. Director General Ian Trethowan, according to the *Salisbury Herald*, said they 'were no different from others Mr Young had done from such places as Russia and the Middle East'. Well at least we weren't being ignored, and that's always a good starting point.

The one trip which we did make on Wednesday was to see the studio from which we would be doing the programmes. Broadcasting House in Salisbury is in a very pleasant setting indeed. Surrounded by fields, it is, in its tranquillity, a far cry from London's Broadcasting House with the nose to tail traffic of Portland Place immediately outside it. Not to mention the pickets of course. The Rhodesian staff were very courteous and helpful. They were also very suspicious. In fact, we were all very conscious of this the whole time we were in Salisbury. The whites' attitude was almost as though we had gone there specifically to attack them. From our point of view all we wanted was to present two balanced and fair-minded programmes. However, we had little time to spend even looking at the broadcasting facilities, important though they were. We hurried back to the hotel, where we were joined by the BBC man in Salisbury, Ian Mills, who had proved a tower of strength to us, and began work. As the sun poured down invitingly from outside we spent the day slaving over hot typewriters in my hotel room.

It was the early hours of the following morning before we decided we could do no more. Our first programme from Zimbabwe was on Thursday 9 August 1979 and, as I sat in the studio waiting to begin, I couldn't help reflecting that it was a very significant date for me. Exactly thirty years before, to the very day, I had been sitting in the BBC's studios near Piccadilly Circus waiting to begin a different kind of broadcast. It was my first ever, in which I was to play the piano and sing four songs. Had anyone told me then that, thirty years on to the day I would be sitting in a studio in Salisbury, Zimbabwe Rhodesia, waiting to interview the Prime Minister, I would never have believed them.

My opening announcement reflected both the weather and the deceptive tranquillity of the area surrounding Broadcasting House. I said, 'Today we have the first of two programmes coming live from Zimbabwe. The sun is shining, the weather's beautiful, and if you didn't know that such a thing existed it would be hard to believe that a bitter, savage war is going on only a very few miles away.' Within a matter of minutes I was talking to Lieutenant General Peter Walls, the man responsible for the security forces. I asked him how far one could go out of Salisbury in absolute safety. The General speedily brought the war into very close focus by saying, 'Well, I would say you can't go anywhere in this country in absolute safety.' He admitted that he was fighting a war which he could possibly contain, but which he knew he could never win. I remember thinking that the atmosphere in the studio during the two days of broadcasts was rather like being present at a death, with every member of the family blaming every other member for causing it. The general tenor of argument from the white people I interviewed was that they realized that something should have been done for the blacks years ago, but that at least something was being done now. Yet even as they spoke to me their fear of the future was obvious. They knew that anything being done was far too little, and years too late. As for the blacks to whom I talked, they knew that whatever happened it would be many years before life really got any better for them. A white educationalist told me that, 'As black aspirations have grown they have been met', while in almost the same breath admitting that only one in five black Africans received a secondary education, and that a whole generation of Africans had grown up without an education at all.

I asked a farmer about the imbalance between black and white in land ownership. Said he, 'There is no racial barrier in the ownership of commercial land.'

Suggesting that there was, I said, 'Presumably in order to buy land you have to have the money with which to buy it.'

Quick as a flash he answered, 'Ah, that's an economic barrier!' I felt rather like a passenger bandying words with the Captain on the bridge of the Titanic.

I asked a black business man how difficult it was for an African to start out in business. How did he raise capital? His name was Mr Mwamuka and he said, 'Raising finance is one of the biggest difficulties in the African community. Finance houses will not let an African have money unless he can produce collateral, and he cannot get collateral until he has some money.'

I spoke to Mrs Esther Rauson, a leading member of the coloured community and a candidate in the elections held the previous April. I asked her how the electoral system worked. Was it in fact a case of white M.P.s for white people and black M.P.s for black people? She agreed that that was the way it worked out in practice. Pushing my luck a bit I asked her where, as a coloured woman, that put her. 'Ah,' said she, 'according to the Rhodesian Constitution, for voting purposes I'm white.'

'I see,' said I, not really seeing at all, 'so blacks are black but coloureds are white.'

'Yes,' said Esther, 'I wasn't allowed to stand in a black constituency so I had to stand in a white constituency. Naturally I didn't get any whites voting for me so that did rather put me in the middle of nowhere.' I felt that, had I been Eric Morecambe at the time, I might well have said, 'There's no answer to that.'

At the end of the first day's programme I was to interview the Prime Minister. I had already been told that, before he came in, the studio would first have to be inspected by one of his security guards. The studio door opened and in came a short, slightly built, almost delicate looking young black man. He was carrying what looked like a Ken Dodd tickling stick, and he was presumably looking for explosives, although I've made a lifelong habit of not blowing myself up. He moved around the studio flicking things with his tickling stick, and eventually arrived at my desk. He never spoke a word but had a good look at me. Then, even as I continued broadcasting, he flicked around my feet, around the legs of my trousers, and under my chair. Seemingly satisfied he exited. After the programme I said to Harry, 'He didn't seem heavy enough to be a security guard.'

Said Harry, 'You should have seen the ones next door. About fifteen of 'em. All built like bloody brick outhouses.'

In came the Prime Minister, Bishop Muzorewa. He was polite and reasonable, until I moved him on to the suggestions and statements which had been coming out of the Commonwealth conference in Lusaka. I asked him what would be his feelings if the British Prime Minister, Mrs Thatcher, were to suggest new elections for Zimbabwe Rhodesia. This would be, he said, 'an insult to the electorate who braved strongly the threat of death as they went to vote for their Government.' And when I persisted with my questions he, at one stage, retorted, 'I am getting sick and tired of talking about what she said and what you said. I am now waiting to see, in black and white, exactly what is required of us.'

I felt we all knew that, in time, what would be required would be new elections; which the Bishop would lose.

I interviewed a man called Cephas Msipa. He had been the assistant editor of the *Zimbabwe Times* until he was arrested and detained. I asked him why he had been arrested. He said, 'I don't know why. They never give reasons. All I know is that I was detained.' I had introduced Mr Msipa as being 'a former official of Joshua Nkomo's ZAPU Party.' Only after the broadcast was Harry able to tell me that, at the very mention of the words Nkomo and ZAPU, all the white Rhodesians in the control box gasped out loud. Harry said he had never heard such a reaction. Such was the overpowering air of fear and suspicion that we were all glad to come to the end of the second programme. No sooner had our signature tune died away than we were delighted to hear the voice of then Managing Director Radio – now boss of BBC Television – Aubrey Singer, booming down the line from London. He said, 'You dodged all the pitfalls, avoided all the booby traps. Well done, and warmest congratulations from everyone at all levels here.'

We returned to the hotel and, after two days of very heavy, serious, and sometimes downright gloomy broadcasting, were rewarded with a moment of almost classic Goon-type humour. As we walked up the steps and then across the hotel foyer the tannoy boomed out, 'Will Mr Young please telephone his butcher immediately.' We all fell about laughing as I said, 'Well, I know I haven't paid last week's bill, but this is ridiculous!' I went over to the reception desk to discover that, by the most extraordinary coincidence, my butcher from London just happened to be in Salisbury at the same time as us.

OK, so it's a cliché, but it really *is* a small world.

Soon it was time to fly out. John Gurnett, with experience gained from his 'recce' trip, had briefed us about take-off from Salisbury. He said their pilot had warned them that immediately after take-off, there would be a very sharp banking manoeuvre followed by a steep climb at full power. 'If we don't do that,' said the Captain, 'we stand a good chance of getting shot down.' I wasn't really looking forward to that too much. However, I needn't have worried. We flew out of Salisbury in a Viscount which was so ancient that, if you'd suggested anything like a sharp bank and full power climb to the Captain, he'd have fallen about laughing. Instead, we did a gentle take-off and then climbed in what seemed like never ending circles until we reached 16,000 feet. Considered then to be out of range of ground to air missiles we set course for Johannesburg. Only later, incidentally, did the Captain conversationally tell us that the guerillas below needed only one vital piece of equipment to make their missiles operational up to 20,000 feet. He went on to express the opinion that 'one of these days some airline captain is going to have a rather nasty surprise.' He did have the decency to wait until we were well on our way to Johannesburg before he told us!

I cannot say that the Zimbabwe programmes had been enjoyable to do, but we had no doubt that they had been well worthwhile.

11- O.B.E.

Wednesday 24 October 1979 saw the return of Dr Hugh Jolly, and if you think I'm going to apologize for mentioning Hugh again you are quite wrong. We had long known him both as one of our favourite people, and a quite exceptional broadcaster. We were now to discover that he was also a man of the highest courage, grit and tenacity. Exactly twenty-eight days before, on 26 September, Hugh had been struck down by a heart attack. Indeed, but for the quite exceptional circumstances in which it occurred, he might never have survived. We, of course, were just thankful that he was still of this world. We were quite certain he would not be 'of this programme' just twenty-eight days later. Hugh had very different ideas.

'Don't you dare rule me out,' he said on the telephone, 'I shall be there.' And, sure enough, he was. As a matter of fact, he even managed to give us a good laugh with the story of how it happened.

He was chairing a meeting at his own Charing Cross Hospital. He explained to us that sometimes, when the going gets a bit heavy at such meetings, he has a habit of leaning back in his chair and closing his eyes. Still awake of course, but giving the impression that he might be having a little cat nap. So, when it happened on this occasion no one immediately paid any particular attention. Just Hugh nodding off they thought. But far from just nodding off, Hugh was actually having a heart attack! His whole team immediately went into action – they are very used to resuscitating babies – and straightaway they breathed and worked his heart for him, though it was fifteen minutes before it beat on its own. A very close call indeed. As Hugh told us, 'If you're going to have a heart attack, have it when you're surrounded by doctors, trained in resuscitation.'

A few weeks later I was attending a supper party at the home of our Managing Director, Aubrey Singer, which was being given in honour of a group of Chinese Radio and Television officials who were visiting the BBC. I was about to be given an example of subtle Chinese humour. And in a foreign language at that.

I was making polite conversation, through an interpreter, with a non-English-speaking Chinese gentleman. He already knew all about the 'JY Programme', having been shown around Broadcasting House earlier in the day while I was actually on the air. He had also been told that I was just beginning this book and was now asking some quite personal questions about my private life.

'Was I married?' he enquired through the interpreter.

'No', I replied. 'I have been married, but at present I am single.'

He thought for a little while, then another flurry of Chinese followed. 'Did I have any girl friends?' asked the interpreter.

'Yes, I have quite a few girl friends', I replied, wondering what was coming next.

Another pause for thought, then the impassive, Chinese face lit up with a huge smile. He literally bounced up and down with excitement as he rattled out the Chinese joke. I waited, spellbound, for it to arrive. Said the interpreter, 'He's just thought of the perfect title for your book: "The Current Affairs of Jimmy Young"!' When I, too, roared with laughter it was quite clear that I had made his day. As a matter of fact I remember thinking at the time that, even for an Englishman it wouldn't have been a bad play on words, but for a non-English-speaking Chinese it was absolutely brilliant. Incidentally, should you wonder why the book *isn't* called 'The Current Affairs of Jimmy Young' it is because, I'm glad to be able to say, my private life is now so content that the only current affairs I have are of the broadcasting variety.

One memory I particularly treasure is of a lunch at the Savoy Hotel in London. I was to receive an award of which I am very proud.

I was one of twelve people named 'Men of the Year' by R.A.D.A.R., The Royal Association for Disability and Rehabilitation. Two other 'names' among the twelve were Sebastian Coe and J. P. R. Williams. But what really made the occasion for me was meeting people who had performed the most astonishing acts of courage and endurance, without any thought whatsoever for their own safety. People who have triumphed over the most severe physical and mental handicaps and come through to lead rewarding lives.

One of the twelve was a young army officer who had only recently suffered the most appalling injuries in Northern Ireland. He had lost an arm and a leg, but he was clearly going to walk, unaided, from his table to the rostrum to collect his award, no matter what the pain. Agonizingly slowly he made his way from his seat. He almost fell several times but he made it there and back. We had all held our breath. As he reached his seat we sighed with relief and every single person in the room leaped to their feet to applaud his magnificent courage. J. P. R., a man who has demonstrated his courage on the rugby field often enough, turned to me and said, 'Doesn't that make you feel bloody humble?'

Yes, it did.

A wonderful year for me ended with the event with which I began this book, my visit to Buckingham Palace to collect the O.B.E. Despite all my experience of meeting 'important people' no one could have been more nervous than I on 4 December 1979.

First came the visit to Moss Bros, to collect the morning suit and topper. Then, suitably rigged out, it was off to the Palace.

Upon entering, your name is checked on the list. Then you're politely, but firmly, segregated into pens. The C.B.E.s and the O.B.E.s in one. The M.B.E.s in another and so on. As you're ushered in, a gentleman sticks a little hook on your lapel. The hook on which, later, will be hung the gong. Eventually, after about an hour in our case, the call comes. Your names are read out, and you join what is, in effect, a very long crocodile file. Somewhere in the distance you faintly hear a band playing. In my case, and it's one of those silly little details that will stick in my mind for ever of course, the first tune I was able to make out was, 'Some day My Prince Will Come'. You slowly shuffle forward, literally just a few inches at a time. There is much nervous conversation and a little giggling. There's a great deal of fiddling with the hired plumes.

Eventually you arrive at the door of the room. Up in the musicians gallery you see the orchestra quietly playing familiar melodies from light opera. On the dais below is the Queen. The room is packed with the friends and relatives of those about to be honoured. Eventually you realize that you are next. Last minute instructions are issued as you stand, nervously, in the doorway. 'When the person before you leaves the Queen walk straight forward. Then, when you are level with the Queen turn to face her. Bow. Then walk towards her until you are close enough for the medal to be easily put on to the hook. Do not speak unless spoken to. The Queen will then shake your hand. When she has done so take three paces back, bow, right turn, and march out.' Sounds easy enough, doesn't it? Your name is called. Off you go. You are immediately conscious that every head in the room has swivelled in your direction. You feel every eye in the place staring at you. Instantly your mind goes a complete blank. Or, at any rate, mine did. Walking, something you've been doing perfectly adequately for the past fifty years or so, suddenly becomes the most difficult thing in the world. You are quite certain you're going to fall over. It's rather like one of those nightmares in which you are trying to run, but your legs won't move. Eventually you arrive at the dais and look up at the Queen. You hope you are near enough for her to put the O.B.E. on the hook without herself falling over. Oh, the agony, not to mention the Tower of London, if she did. 'Mr Young,' said the Queen, 'I quite like that little argument you have with Mr

Wogan in the mornings.' Before I knew it, and still in a daze, I was on my way.

Out into the courtyard to face the newspaper photographers. 'Just one more, Jim', the cry of photographers everywhere, went on for twenty minutes or so, and then it was the turn of BBC Television to ask if I would do a quick interview for their news bulletin.

'Of course, it would be a pleasure', I said. To be immediately confronted by a stupid question written by some bright spark in the Television Centre.

'It's been said that you get important people on your programme because you ask soft questions. Is that true?' asked the interviewer.

I thought, 'this is just about all I needed this morning', and said, 'You don't have to go red in the face to ask hard questions, and you don't get headline quotes out of politicians by asking *soft* questions.' Needless to say, they didn't use that bit on the news.

The next day was to be quite an eventful one for me as well. Some years before, I had decided that it would help to establish the show as a serious, credible, current affairs programme if I stopped singing. I had taken that decision after a great deal of thought, not because my voice had packed up on me, but because I knew that there was some jealousy surrounding the success of the programme, and that there were still people anxious to knock us. I realized that the feeling that I still really belonged in Light Entertainment gave them a weapon to use against us. There was, of course, no logical reason on earth why it should. Nevertheless, Harry Walters and I talked about it and came to the decision that, for a while at any rate, it would be better if I gave up singing. To tell the truth, I was so interested in what I was now doing, that I didn't miss it very much anyway. Then, quite out of the blue, in 1979 something happened. Our music producer at the time, in other words the person who chooses the records for the programme, was a very bright lady called Ann Mann. One day she asked me, 'I don't suppose you'd fancy doing a singing programme for Christmas Day, would you?'

I thought to myself; well, Jimbo, this is it. Crunch time. Do you risk the credibility of the programme which is so important to you, or have you now achieved sufficient status that the occasional singing programme would do no harm? Once again, Harry and I went into a huddle, together with Ann and Head of Radio 2, Geoffrey Owen. We decided that, provided I didn't do it too often, it was a risk worth taking. Accordingly, on 5 December 1979 I did the morning 'JY Prog' and then, at 2.30 p.m., went to studio 6 at Maida Vale to record a programme of Christmas songs. Ann had engaged Neil Richardson to conduct the BBC Radio Orchestra, and also appearing on the programme were the Mike Sammes Singers. We were all old friends and had worked together many, many times over the years. They gave me a wonderful welcome and did their best to make me feel thoroughly at home. The atmosphere in the studio was lovely. Nevertheless, walking in cold from the street, as they say in the trade, to do a one hour singing programme was, to say the least, a bit of a challenge. In the event it all went very well. Harry and Ann, who were in the control box, were clearly tickled pink. To round it off, after I had finished the final song, the orchestra gave me their verdict. They rapped on their music stands with their bows, the musicians' equivalent of a standing ovation. I was very moved. However, as I drove home, my mind told me something very clearly. Although I would quite enjoy doing three or four singing programmes a year, if that was what the BBC wanted, never again would singing be my prime love. I was now quite firmly rooted in the current affairs area, where I had always really wanted to be.

February 1980 brought one of the most extraordinary, and bizarre happenings of my entire life. Friends of mine had invited my girlfriend, Alicia, and me to spend a couple of weeks' holiday with them in Florida. We flew over on 2 February, and were met at Miami airport by Derek Boulton and his wife, Siv.

We settled into the apartment which they were kindly lending us, and spent a blissful first week. It was in the second week that it all happened. Derek received a telephone call from the New York office of an English newspaper. He was asked if he knew where I was. Quite unthinkingly he said, 'Yes, he's next door.' The caller then told him that he had received a cable from head office in London which read, 'Great interest here in JY and girlfriend sunning themselves in Florida.'

You could have knocked us over with the proverbial feather. We had been together for years, attending official dinners and functions. There had never been any secrets about us whatsoever. Derek said to me, 'Come in and use my phone. We'll speak to him and I'm sure it will quietly go away.' I was not so sure. However, I agreed to give it a go. I explained the situation and, sure enough, Derek seemed to be right. Indeed, later in the day he received another call from the journalist saying, 'What a nice man Mr Young is. Will you thank him for phoning and explaining?'

Said Derek, 'See, I told you so.' I still had my doubts.

We were to fly back overnight on Friday 15 February. Derek and Siv drove us to Miami airport. Derek went to park the car. Siv, Alicia and I walked on into the airport. Suddenly all hell broke loose. As we walked slowly towards the checking-in queue, a photographer jumped out from behind a pillar. He whizzed around and around us, a whirling dervish, taking pictures. Siv and Alicia made for the ladies loo and, looking in that direction, I could see two pale faces peering round the partially opened door. A huge Englishman detached himself from the front of the checking-in queue. 'Having problems, Jim?' he asked.

'Not really', said I.

He walked up to the cameraman. 'If you don't stop this right now,' he said, 'I'll bloody flatten you.' The cameraman took the hint. I was shepherded through to Customs by three large Brits. Alicia, by Siv and Derek. Looking back it's possible to see the funny side, but at the time it was anything but funny.

Our flight home was to complete a thoroughly bad day. We hit some of the worst turbulence I have ever encountered. Crockery flew everywhere. There were moans, groans, the occasional shriek, and the sounds of people being ill. In the middle of it all the Captain spoke to reassure us. He said, 'I'm sorry about this extreme turbulence, but I would just like to assure you that you are flying in a *very* safe aircraft.' That was just about all we needed. I was now absolutely convinced that the wings were about to fall off.

Monday 18 February saw the Jim and Alicia Miami love story in banner headlines in one national newspaper. Alan Monahan, now BBC Radio's Senior Publicity Officer, immediately advised me that, much though we didn't want to do so, the way to stop the story from dragging on for ever, was to call a midday press conference. This we did. I've never seen so many reporters and photographers in one place at the same time as were gathered in the St George's Hotel in London that day. I pointed out that there had never been any secrecy about Alicia and myself, and that all our friends had known of our feelings for each other for many, many years. The writers scribbled, the photographers snapped, and everybody went away happy – the story had suddenly ceased to be news.

12-Telethon

Just when I had given up singing, I found myself back singing again. This time, though, with a difference. Terry Wogan and I, would you believe, were to record a duet. It was a song especially written for a record sponsored by a brewery. Our particular epic was called 'Two Heads Are Better Than One'. Thought I at the time; when the other head belongs to Wogan I'm not so sure!

Like everyone who appears on television and radio I get involved in a lot of charity work, but when Thames Television approached me about the Telethon I knew somehow or other I had to find time to do it. This was Britain's first ever Telethon and seemed to me to be a wonderful way of raising money for deserving causes.

Since the programme was not networked, and was therefore seen only by viewers in the Thames Television area, perhaps I should briefly explain what a Telethon is.

In simple terms, it is a marathon television programme, designed to raise as much money as possible for charity. Money is telephoned in and 'pledged' on the banks of telephones manned by volunteers. Artists involved donate their services free of charge. Thames planned to scrap all their regular programmes for the night of Thursday 2 October 1980. The Telethon would start at 7 p.m. and, with only a thirty-minute break for 'News at Ten', would run continuously until 3 a.m.

on Friday morning. It would re-start at 3 p.m. on Friday afternoon and finish at 7 p.m. on Friday evening, 3 October. All
told, eleven-and-a-half hours of Telethon. I did the morning
radio programme as usual, then headed for the Wembley Conference Centre. Of the three co-presenters only Rolf Harris had
introduced Telethons before. For Joan Shenton and myself it
was a leap into the unknown; however, I was greatly looking
forward to it. The main reasons were that, with a show of such
length there could obviously be no set script. Furthermore, the
show had been subdivided into hours one, two, three, and so
on, with guests slotted in according to which hour they had
indicated they could make. Joan, Rolf and I had then been
pencilled in to interview them according to whoever was felt
to be most suitable. It seemed to me that there wasn't the
slightest chance this system would work out in practice. It
looked nice and tidy on paper, but obviously some guests
would be early, some late, some would be held up in traffic,
some might even never get there at all. I figured therefore,
that with no script, and no set pattern, I was looking at something very similar to what I do for a living two hours a day,
five days a week. In the event that was the case.

I was also lucky enough again to be surrounded by friendly
faces. Neil Richardson was musical director. Kenny Ball, another old mate, was there with his Jazzmen. Charles Thompson, who was once chief researcher on my radio programme,
was there in his capacity as entertainment producer.

It's difficult to give you a complete list of the stars who had
volunteered to give their services free of charge, so many were
there; but they included, Bob Hope, Cliff Richard, Sammy
Davis Jnr, Stevie Wonder, Roger Moore, Michael Caine, Diana
Ross, Tommy Cooper, Frankie Vaughan, Lionel Blair, Faith
Brown, Henry Cooper, The Drifters, Hinge and Bracket, Fran-
kie Howard, Danny La Rue, Spike Milligan, Sir John Mills,
Leo Sayer and Norman Wisdom.

The atmosphere backstage was electric. Two hundred telephones had been specially installed on raised banks at the back
of the stage at the Wembley Conference Centre. These would
be manned throughout the entire show by volunteers taking
incoming telephone calls and pledges of money. Stars would

do their act, and then go to man the phones for as long as they were able to stay with us. Came 7 p.m. and away we went.

Rolf, Joan and I explained what a Telethon is all about. We pointed out that we wanted *all* our phones ringing *all* of the time. We even sang a song about it, 'You gotta make those telephones ring'. As though by magic, and to the delight of all of us, they did. The Drifters sang a song. Joan did an interview with Cliff Richard. Leo Sayer turned up, Kenny Ball played. Bernie Winters introduced the professional darts tournament. Of yes, you get a bit of everything in a Telethon! I introduced a piece of film in which I interviewed the prettiest little girl you could ever wish to see, suffering from brain damage due to the lack of a piece of medical equipment when she was born. The night's Telethon was all about helping just such children. Max Bygraves came along, as did Marti Webb, Faith Brown and Frank Ifield. Paul Daniels did a magic act with Susan Hampshire. Bob Hope popped in for five minutes, courtesy of satellite television. And we weren't even up to 10 o'clock yet! Best of all, the phones never stopped.

The digits in shining lights behind Rolf, Joan and myself had begun to move. Every so often one of us would cry, 'Let's have a new total.' The audience, packed into the Wembley Conference Centre, called the numbers out with us as we read them in reverse order, right to left.

What had, at 7 o'clock, been 0000000, by 7.10 p.m. was, in reverse order, 00051 – £15,000. We were on our way.

We called for a new total just before we went off the air to make way for 'News at Ten'. With us the audience roared out, 000,052 – £250,000! And the beautiful thing about it was that it wasn't all coming in huge cheques from giant corporations. Far from it. Most of the donations were coming in £1s, £5s and so on. As we repeatedly said on the show, 'We don't mind how much, or how little, you give. Nothing's too big and nothing's too small.' The entertainment rolled on, and the money rolled in. Some viewers were incredibly, beautifully, generous. A young lady, called Susan Francis, who was going on holiday had had the misfortune to break both her legs and couldn't go. So she donated her entire holiday money, £750, to help the Telethon. A marvellous gesture. And only one of many. Amazingly, as the pledges flowed in we realized that almost the entire audience was staying with us. They were hooked. The Telethon was proving a major success. By 12.32 a.m. we had raised half a million pounds. We closed for the night at 3.17 a.m. with a final total that read, £600,089. Not bad for a night's work.

Now came the hard bit, for me anyway. Thames Television had booked me in at The White House Hotel in Regents Park, near Broadcasting House. I was driven there from Wembley and staggered into bed at 4.30 a.m. on the morning of Friday 3 October. Two-and-a-half hours later I was up and reading all the papers, ready for John Gurnett's telephone call from the Beeb at 8 a.m. We set up the programme as usual, and I was able to amble gently down the road to work. At midday it was off to the Wembley Conference Centre again.

When I reached Wembley it was to be told that the telephones had been ringing all night, and all Friday morning. Up went the cry, 'Let's have a new total.'

The audience, and the Wembley Conference Centre had never been anything other than packed, roared with us as Joan, Rolf and I announced that it was £725,000. The magic moment we had all been waiting for came at 6.05 p.m. exactly, when, to the biggest roar so far, and tumultuous applause that carried on for minutes, we read out 000,000,1. Yes, we'd made it. Overnight we had raised one million pounds. We ended, worn out but happy at 7 p.m. The total then was £1,108,467. And the phones were still ringing. Only later did we learn that we might even have raised considerably more money but, despite having 200 lines, the poor old switchboard just couldn't cope. Apparently at one stage during the night it packed up altogether. Still, we were happy with what we'd got.

The press coverage, of course, was massive. The *Evening News* of 3 October headlined, 'With a Thon In Their Hearts'. Other papers spoke of 'Telethon's Way To The Nation's Heart'. Even the carpers found carping difficult. It's not easy to knock something that gave Thames even higher viewing figures than normal, and raised one-and-a-quarter-million pounds for charity in just twenty-four hours.

During the latter half of 1980 Radio 2 had acquired a new Controller. Douglas Muggeridge had moved to Bush House to become Managing Director of the BBC's prestigious External Services, while Charles McLelland had been promoted to become Deputy Managing Director Radio. Both had previously held the post of Controller Radio 2. You will see, therefore, that it is one of the key jobs in the BBC structure.

Into it came David Hatch. A young man, in his early forties, David has nevertheless crammed in an enormous amount of show business and broadcasting experience of almost incredible diversity. While at Cambridge he was in the 1963 vintage year Cambridge Footlights, with John Cleese, Graham Chapman, Bill Oddie and Tim Brooke-Taylor. He worked as a radio actor, did a spell at *Radio Times*, and was a researcher on 'In Town Tonight', eventually becoming a producer, dedicated to revitalizing radio entertainment. You will have gathered that he is something of a dynamo. Naturally, he would want to make changes.

The headlines once again told the story: 'Major shake up for Radio 2', 'Massive Shake Up', 'All Change at the Beeb', 'New Chief Shakes up Radio 2'. When the dust had settled just about the only two bottoms still sitting on their original chairs were Wogan's and mine. As a headline in the *Edinburgh Evening News* put it, 'Wogan and JY Survive'.

13-Tokyo

The Spring of 1981 saw us once again making preparations for overseas travel. We had been discussing the possibilities of mounting some live programmes from Japan, and we presented our ideas to the new Controller of Radio 2.

To our delight he gave us his approval. The motor industry seemed the obvious place to begin. For some time the Japanese had been a thorn niggling in the side of European motor manufacturers. They were now beginning to niggle America as well. It seemed to us that an on the spot look at a leading Japanese motor manufacturer might throw some light on the runaway success of their industry, and the problems being encountered by ours. To present a balanced picture we suggested to British Leyland that we should mount an outside broadcast from Longbridge on our return from Japan. Unfortunately, they declined to allow us to do so.

Not that the programmes were to be exclusively about motor cars. The electronics industry was another area on which the Japanese had concentrated and obtained a dominant role. In addition we arranged to talk about Japanese culture, housing, education, the role of women in society, crime, law and order and Japanese foreign policy. We were well aware that these would be the hardest overseas programmes we had ever attempted. First because we were aiming to do three full days of programmes instead of the usual two, and second because of the immense distance involved. Eighteen hours in the air is, to say the very least, not my idea of a fun flight. We relied on the format which, by now, had served us so well in the Soviet Union, Egypt, Israel and Zimbabwe. Harry immediately fired off a telex to the BBC Office in Tokyo. Our man there, to whom I had spoken on the Prog many times but had never met, was Bob Friend. When eventually I *did* meet Bob I was to discover that he was a large, outgoing man with a great sense of humour. A fine journalist, he also had the knack of recruiting the right kind of help, enlisting Fuyoko Nishisato.

Would she turn out to be another 'fixer' like Sana-el-Saed of, by now legendary, President Sadat fame, we wondered! Had we known Bob better, the question would not have arisen. She did.

Researcher Mike Rhodes (fortunately a bit of a nut about flying so he didn't mind doing the journey twice) and engineer, John Ford, flew over to do a 'recce'. John returned to announce that he was happy with the engineering scene. We were all delighted with the list of people Mike and Fuyoko had compiled for me to interview on the programmes. It looked as though, with a bit of luck and a great deal of hard work, we might be on to another winner. Again the hard graft of preparation began. Every evening and every weekend, right up to the off, we all worked at our individual research, pooling the results. These were typed up, then altered and typed up again. And again. And again. I somehow got the feeling, and I don't think I was far wrong, that by the time we reached the point of flying out on these foreign trips, our office secretaries were damned glad to see the back of us for a few days.

Friday 22 May was the day we departed for the Land of the Rising Sun. I began the programme, as usual, at 10 o'clock. The one difference from a normal morning was that, instead of running on through to midday, we had to leap out of the studio at 11 a.m. and be in a car at 5 minutes past 11 in order to get to Heathrow Airport in time to catch the British Airways flight to Tokyo. Colin Berry, the excellent broadcaster in his own right who normally stands in for me on these occasions, was to hold the fort for the last hour of the programme. Colin duly arrived and so did the 11 o'clock news. One minute to throw on the jacket and tie and pick up the case. Then it was a quick scuttle along the corridors of Broadcasting House and into the waiting car. Tokyo, here we come. Well, not quite. First I got a foretaste of a possible future disaster. Just as we were passing through customs at Heathrow I heard a sudden shriek. I turned.

Standing about two feet away from me was a short, fat, almost square woman. She threw herself upon me, at the same time shrieking, 'My God it's him. It's Jimmy Young. I'm coming to work for you when I get back from Los Angeles.'

'Work where?' I cried weakly. To my horror she named the road in which I live.

My God, I thought, I'm going to be back to the lady in the red coat and me nude in the hall again in a minute.

As the team pulled her off me I said, 'How long are you going to Los Angeles for?'

'Two months' she shouted as she struggled to get at me again. I think I'm going to have to move y'know.

Take off time of BA 05 from Terminal 3 at London Heathrow was 13.10. We were to fly to Tokyo Narita Airport via Anchorage. Mike Rhodes had warned us in advance about Anchorage. Even so it still came as a bit of a surprise. Having flown for eight hours from London you eventually arrive at Alaska. Nobody really wants to be there, but it's necessary if you want to get to Japan. And it's not just flights to and from Japan, of course. It's flights to and from just about everywhere. Anchorage is the Clapham Junction of the Airways.

Everybody's flown for hours and realizes only too well that they're still only about half-way from their destination, so it's full of half asleep, jet-lagged people walking aimlessly about bumping into each other. Not only don't they know what time it is, a lot of 'em don't even know what day it is. Or care. And that, I may say, included me. Just about the only reason I can think of for going to Anchorage is to see the bear. He's about nine feet tall. White. Huge claws, ferocious teeth. Stuffed and in a glass case, I'm happy to say. Once you've seen him, that's it. You've done Anchorage.

Thank God, I thought when, at last, we reached Tokyo. Now for a bath and bed. Little did I know. Used to the fifteen-minute journey from London's Heathrow Airport to my home, I had not realized that Tokyo's Narita Airport is sixty kilometres from Tokyo. Not only that, if you have a favourite story of being caught in a traffic jam, forget it. Until you've seen Tokyo you ain't seen nothin'. It was not till some time later when I asked how long it usually took to get to Tokyo airport that I was told, 'Well, you *can* do it in an hour and a half – but on the other hand it's not unknown for it to take *four* and a half hours!' In fact very early on in our short stay in Tokyo a hardened resident told us, 'Don't worry if you're late for an appointment, nobody else does. With traffic like this it's impossible to estimate how long any journey's going to take!'

At 3.30 p.m. on Saturday afternoon Japanese local time, we set out from Narita Airport for Tokyo. The next two hours were hell on wheels. Eighteen hours in an aeroplane is bad enough, but spending a further two hours in a continuous traffic jam finishes you off. Suffice it to say that when my left leg began to jerk up and down and my hands to twitch, I felt perhaps it was all beginning to get to me.

We arrived at the New Otani Hotel in Tokyo at about 5.45 p.m. None of us felt too well, but never have I seen Harry look so ill. We were very relieved when he announced his intention of retiring to bed immediately. The rest of us dumped our bags in our rooms, had a shower and a light meal, and then did exactly the same.

Once again, as in Zimbabwe, we had struck lucky with our timing. Subsequent to our decision to come to Japan, something had happened which was to make our programmes even more topical. The E.E.C. and Japan had decided to hold a conference in Brussels that very week, on the vexed question of the limitation of Japanese car imports. Indeed, one of the most important men in Japan, to whom I'd planned to talk on this subject, was due to leave for Brussels on Tuesday 26 May and would have been unable to take part in our programmes. That is why, on Monday afternoon, John Gurnett, Mike Rhodes, Alan Wilson and I, presented ourselves at the Ministry of International Trade and Industry to interview Mr Hashira Amaya, the Vice Minister for International Affairs.

Mr Amaya is a fascinating man, small, impeccably groomed, a wide smile, scrupulously polite, and totally immovable. I won't say that two minutes into the interview I thought I could have saved the E.E.C. Ministers their fares to Brussels, but, when I asked him whether Japan would be prepared to lower the level of their car imports into the E.E.C. and Britain, to equate with the much lower level they had just agreed with the United States of America, he said, 'No.' Not just like that. He used quite a lot of words to say it. However, that's what he meant, and he never really moved from that position. I did get him to agree that forcing in massive Japanese imports was pretty much resented and I suggested that a more agreeable way forward might be to get increasingly involved in joint ventures with the host countries. To build products abroad on a partnership basis, rather than building them totally in Japan and then exporting them. He conceded that, yes, this would be a better way to proceed. My thoughts were, if you can't beat 'em, join 'em. Or at least get 'em to join you.

I was also able to get Mr Amaya to admit something which I had not dreamed of, at least until we got involved in researching these programmes. That is that Japan is not at all the freebooting, totally capitalist, 'Government keep out of the way and let business get on with it' society that it seems to an outsider. Far from it in fact. One of the things I had discovered from my reading, and was also just about to have confirmed, was that Japanese Government Ministries are very much involved in the planning of what happens in Industry. Indeed, it is one of the key points of the whole industrial set up. And MITI (pronounced Meaty), where we were sitting with Mr Amaya, is one of the main planning and co-ordinating organizations. It is no accident that the motor and electronics industries are such important areas for the Japanese. They are for the very simple reason that Government and Industry, the Banks and the Unions, sat down together and jointly decided that they should be. I won't bore you with a blow by blow account of a twenty-four minute interview. However, by patient and probing questioning, I did get Mr Amaya to admit certain things: that Japanese Government, both sides of Industry, and the Banks, try to plan up to twenty-five years ahead; that they sit down together, decide on which industries they are going to concentrate, and then do so; that, having decided their priorities, pressure is brought to bear to give those areas every possible help; that the way is smoothed by such things as cheaper bank loans being made available; that absolutely any priorities needed are granted, ruthlessly if need be; and that Japan *did* practise protectionism to safeguard their own electronics industry against foreign competition. Although Mr Amaya insisted that this practice had ceased in 1974.

He had used the phrase, 'We try to *persuade* people' a great deal. Only one further question was necessary to get a complete picture of the carrot and stick situation: 'What happens if companies don't co-operate with the Government persuasions?' I asked Mr Amaya. 'Does the Government cause companies aggravation if they don't play ball?'

'Yes', said Mr Amaya. He did not bother to elaborate, nor did he need to.

I came away wondering whether there was a message there for us at home.

Also on Monday, I interviewed the fascinating Mr Akio Morita. I say fascinating because it's not very often you get to meet someone who has actually started from scratch an organization as vast and successful as the Sony Corporation. Mr Morita was its co-founder, and is now its Chairman.

Something which emerged from what both Mr Amaya and Mr Morita said, and indeed from all the industrialists to whom we spoke in Japan, is the concept of 'The Family' in Industry. Mr Morita told me that when a new employee joins Sony he is said to have joined the 'Sony Family', with the expectation that he would most probably remain with the same 'Family' for the rest of his working life. The whole concept of 'A job for life' is very strong in Japanese Industry. Indeed, Mr Morita told me that when he went to America in the late Fifties and early Sixties he was absolutely amazed to find that he could actually fire somebody if he wanted to! And when one of his senior executives told him that he wanted to leave Sony to take up a job elsewhere he, Mr Morita, just couldn't believe it!

I asked both Mr Amaya and Mr Morita whether this would apply should Japan suffer a depression and Japanese firms hit hard times. They both insisted that the same conditions would still apply. Mr Morita pointed out that there was nothing legally binding on a firm that this should be the case. Nonetheless his feeling was that in bad times, rather than laying off the work force, the company should suffer the loss of profits themselves. 'After all,' he said, 'the recession is not the workers' fault. The company hired them in the first place, and the company should keep them on the work force until times improve.'

Mind you, as we frequently heard, the concept of 'joining the firm's Family' can be a two-edged sword. Many are the stories of Japanese husbands ending up married to the firm itself. Staggering home with their briefcase at midnight. Getting up at 6 a.m. to begin a new day. Indeed, one Japanese husband, when asked about his priorities, said they were No.1 The Firm, No.2 his mates at work, No.3 the quality of the firm's product, and No.4 his wife and family. I don't think many British wives would be happy to go along with that.

The studio from which I was to broadcast was, as Harry had warned me, the smallest studio in which I'd ever worked. It was also boiling hot, and nobody could lay a hand on a fan anywhere. However, it was to be home for the next three days, so there wasn't a lot of point in complaining. Fortunately John Ford and Alan Wilson were there, and these are the moments when you utter a prayer of thanks for the expertise of the BBC Engineering Department. I don't mean to suggest that Japanese engineers are incompetent, far from it, but, having worked together in foreign parts over the years, John and Alan instinctively knew how to make me feel comfortable and confident. Within fifteen minutes, they had done it. They have this ability to go into a studio, be it in the Soviet Union, Egypt, Israel, Zimbabwe, Japan, or the Moon I'm quite sure, with a minimum command of the local language, and within a quarter of an hour have the local technicians eating out of their hands, and the whole studio as comfortable as though we were all in Broadcasting House in London. As a man who can't mend a fuse I have the greatest possible admiration for them.

The time difference between London and Tokyo was eight hours so, as the hands of the two clocks on my studio wall came up to 6 p.m. Tokyo time, 10 a.m. London time, Colin Berry played the signature tune in London and away we went.

I spoke to Dr Saburo Okita, a former Foreign Minister and now Chief Trade Negotiator at the Defence Ministry. We talked about Japanese Foreign Policy and Defence. Defence, and nuclear weapons, are very ticklish subjects in Japan. Ironically, Japan has been under pressure from America to contribute more money towards defence. The theory being that as long as Japan can shelter behind America, and especially America's nuclear power, she can get away with spending less money on defence, and therefore have more available to fuel the super efficient Japanese industrial effort. The very industrial effort causing some of America's problems! As for nuclear weapons themselves, Japan, as you can imagine, having had first-hand experience at being on the receiving end, wants as little to do with nuclear weapons as possible. Hence, when we were there one of the major issues being discussed in the news was whether, when they were berthed in Japanese ports, American warships were carrying nuclear weapons. I asked Mr Okita about this. He replied that there was really no way of knowing one way or the other whether they did. The Americans always denied that their ships were carrying nuclear weapons, and the Japanese had no right to search them. Impasse.

The Assistant Managing Editor of the *Mainichi* newspaper came in to talk about housing. Tokyo housing, to European eyes, is absolutely incredible. The reason is that the whole city had to be completely rebuilt on two occasions. In 1923/24 following a disastrous earthquake, and again after World War II.

On both occasions, it was done without adequate planning in the haste to get the economy on the move again. Everything was sacrificed to industrial growth. The result, which strikes you forcibly as you drive in from the airport, is one of the unloveliest housing scenes anywhere in the world. Big factories, little houses, and medium-sized office blocks, all crammed together in one unholy mess. In fact, the congestion of traffic, housing and people is so severe that the Government is seriously considering a plan to move Tokyo somewhere else and start all over again!

After our first programme was over, NHK brought it to a delightful close by breaking into spontaneous applause for our whole team at the end of the concluding signature tune. They followed this by announcing that they were taking us out for a celebratory meal. We had a superb evening. Our hosts were absolutely charming, and the meal was delicious. There was only one small surprise. Inscrutable as ever, the Japanese took us out to a Chinese restaurant!

Lunchtime on Wednesday brought good news. Aubrey Singer, who was helping the BBC Symphony Orchestra to enjoy a highly acclaimed tour of the Far East, happened to be in Tokyo and he offered to take us to lunch. Over a tasty helping of prawns in a restaurant in the grounds of the hotel, we were delighted to hear Aubrey say that London, to whom he had talked late the previous night, were highly delighted with the first programme. When you're thousands of miles away from base it's always good for morale to hear that the first helping has gone down well.

The next day we took our first look at the Nissan Motor Company when I interviewed Mr Mitsuya Goto, General Manager Public Affairs, of their International Division. I think I should make it clear that when I write of things like industrial relations in Japanese industry, I am not commenting on whether Japanese industrial practice would work in the UK, I am just reporting either what I saw, or what was said to me.

On the subject of trades unions, for instance, I put it to Mr Goto that, in the Nissan Motor Company, trades union officials and management were practically interchangeable. Said Mr Goto, 'That is quite true. Some of our employees might be asked to serve as full-time union officials. Then, at some stage in the future, they could be made managers, or deputy general managers perhaps.'

I asked how the 'Quality Control Circle' concept worked in Japan.

Said Mr Goto, 'This is a grouping of ten to fifteen of our ordinary employees who monitor the quality of the product. In addition, however, once or twice a month, they would stay on after their normal working hours had ended to discuss ways in which they could improve the quality of the product, or perhaps improve the production processes.'

I asked whether they would get paid for the extra time they

put in. 'Only partially,' said Mr Goto, 'they volunteer to do it. You see, when you join a company, you feel you are a member of a family.' Here we go again I thought. I decided to ask Mr Goto to enlarge a bit on family relationships.

'Well,' he said, 'a company like ours would provide housing, whether bachelor quarters or a family apartment, at minimal rent. A bachelor, for instance, would pay rent of about £3.50 per month. Fifty per cent of the cost of meals in the company dining-room would be paid for by the company. The company also pays sixty per cent of our health insurance and medical care.' I said I had heard an extraordinary story that employees tended not to take their holidays at all, or if they did only in single days, because they did not want the company to suffer. Mr Goto agreed that this indeed used to be the case. He went on, 'That is beginning to change with the younger generation of employees. However,' he said, 'most of us in managerial positions are reluctant to take paid holidays. In fact I have accumulated thirty-six days paid holiday.'

'Are you going to take it?' I asked.

'No, I'm much too busy', he said.

One thing I had learned from our research before we came to Tokyo was that Japan is an intensely competitive nation. Once Government and Industry have taken the decision to concentrate on a certain area, let's say motor cars for instance, that will not prevent individual Japanese motor manufacturers being as competitive with each other as they would be with foreign firms.

But nowhere is competition harder, and in some cases more lethal, than in the field of education. It seems a constant fight. First to get to the best pre-nursery school, then the best nursery school, the best elementary, the best junior high and so on. I asked Mr Michio Nagai, a former Minister of Education and now an adviser to the United Nations University, whether the pressure on young children really was enormous.

'Yes, in comparison with most other countries I think so', he said; 'Tokyo University is the educational Mount Fuji of Japan. Every Japanese wants to climb Mount Fuji, so the pressure is very great.'

I had in front of me a clipping from *The Times*. It laid out the day of a Japanese fourteen-year-old. He left home for school at 7.45 a.m., returned home at 4 p.m. and went straight to bed. His parents woke him at 9 p.m. and he had dinner. He then studied through the night until 4 a.m., when he went back to bed for a couple of hours before getting ready for the next day's school. In addition, he received private tuition in mathematics for an extra four hours a week. I asked Mr Nagai whether that was typical of the pressure. He said, 'Well, typical might not be absolutely the correct word. However, I am sure that many people, especially in city areas, are doing exactly the same thing, for the purpose of getting into a better University, and having better employment.'

I quoted an American who said his son had complained that he couldn't play with any of his Japanese school friends because they were all studying until midnight.

'That would be true', said Mr Nagai. He went on, 'In most countries today there is a thing called the Diploma Disease, but in Japan the disease is more acute than anywhere else.'

I asked whether it was these intense pressures which produced the high suicide rate among young Japanese. 'Yes,' said Mr Nagai, 'and not only suicide, they are under so much pressure that some of them become psychologically disturbed.' He concluded, 'It sometimes seems that our people go to school to obtain a better diploma. Whether or not they receive a better education is another matter.'

Thursday brought us to our last programme from Tokyo. My first interview was to be with Mr Masataka Okuma, Deputy Vice President of the Nissan Motor Company. I asked Mr Okuma what he thought were the reasons for the success of the Japanese motor industry. He gave four: quality; high productivity; appropriate marketing policy; and the worldwide move towards smaller cars. On the subject of the proposed Nissan plant in Britain he had the good news and the bad news. The good news was that, if it went ahead, he hoped it would eventually produce 200,000 units per year and employ four to five thousand people. The bad news was the Nissan feasibility study. This indicated that there would be a problem in maintaining the same quality of components that they enjoyed in Japan. Therefore, Nissan would have to speak to the manufacturers so that quality would be improved, and also so that there would be smooth delivery. As he was speaking, I could see the storm cones being hoisted at home. The next day's papers confirmed that they had been. 'Component makers Reject Slur', thundered the *Financial Times*.

Said a senior executive at one prominent component company, 'In general the British component industry is well ahead of the Japanese in the technology it has to offer.' He hastily went on to add, 'I prefer to remain anonymous – because we hope to get some business from Nissan.'

I am often asked whether we ever have any 'hairy' moments on the programme. I usually say 'not really', but I suppose if by 'hairy' one means losing the line to London, then occasionally we do. We had one in Moscow, one in Jerusalem, and were about to have another one right now. 'Losing the line', in layman terms, means that I can no longer communicate with the outside world on the microphone in my studio. It suddenly ceases to work, just like that. This may sound 'hairy', and to an extent it is, but our engineering team is so good that I know if *they* can't put it right there's absolutely nothing that can be done about it anyway. What it does entail, however, is that, provided our engineering talkback facility to London is still working, I have to fast foot it out of my studio and into the outside control box pretty smartish, and continue broadcasting from out there. One quite amusing by-product of this situation concerns our engineer, Alan Wilson. Alan, during this type of broadcast, is in continuous contact with me by talkback from the other side of the soundproof glass. He is also the first man to know if the line has gone down.

Alan is a large man with a quiet, almost shy manner. However, when these moments happen, and as I said we've had a few of them now in different parts of the world, the routine never varies. He puts down the key and shouts at me, 'JIMMY – COME – OUT – HERE – NOW!', very slowly and distinctly. Rather as we Brits try to communicate in a deafening voice with a native of some foreign country whose language we are unable to speak. I then put down the key on my side of the glass, because although I can't talk to the world I can still talk to Alan, and say, equally slowly and loudly, 'ALAN – PLEASE – DON'T – BLOODY – SHOUT!' It never fails. It always gets a laugh, this time from the whole of NHK as well; the tension is gone, and we carry on as normal. I think it's all down to one thing, as I mentioned to Aubrey Singer at lunch, 'Our great strength is that we always operate as a team.'

Said Aubrey, 'That's quite obvious.'

Back in working order again I talked to Mr Shikita, Director of the Asia/Far East Crime Prevention Institute about the very low level of crime in Japan.

I commented on how much more authority, discipline and supervision the Japanese people were prepared to accept, compared with what might be tolerated elsewhere in the world. Police officers tend to be deployed in small 'patches' so they get to know the people in their area particularly well. Officers take turns to check on all the flats, houses and shops in their area. They check on the number of occupants in each building. The householder fills in a 'green card' with details of the family's job, school, car, and whether they have any lodgers. I asked Mr Shikita whether the Tokyo public resented this, pointing out that, in some Western communities, it might be called invasion of privacy. Mr Shikita said, 'Generally the public do not resent it because they know the police will use the information only for their protection.' He went on, 'It is more difficult to commit crime in Japan, because people who notice suspicious happenings report them to the police immediately, and the police react very quickly.' Juvenile crime, he told me, had increased slowly over the past twenty years, but on the other hand adult crime had been decreasing for the last thirty years. Over the last ten years violent crimes like rape and murder had decreased to one fourth of what they had been, while assault and burglary had decreased to one third. 'However,' said Mr Shikita finally, 'we still have sufficient problems to keep ourselves employed.'

I felt that the police in New York or Miami would have been very happy to settle for Mr Shikita's 'sufficient problems'.

We moved on to the role of Japanese women, and I introduced the item by reading part of the lyric of a popular song which had been top of the Japanese hit parade. The song is called, 'Declaration Of An Overbearing Husband' and it lays down certain guide lines for Japanese wives. The lyric says, 'Do not go to bed before I do. Don't get up after I do. Cook good meals. Always look pretty. Keep quiet. Follow me. And if I have a little affair, well, just put up with it.'

I asked Mrs Fukawo, the Associate Editor of Women's Affairs on one of Japan's main newspapers, whether wives really behaved like that. She gave a qualified yes. She said, 'Well, there are not so many women nowadays who do that.' But she agreed that the song had provoked many letters to Japan's leading newspapers, and the odd thing was that most of the letters agreed with the sentiments of the song.

So, the Japanese man would seem to be very much the dominant character. However, when it comes to running the home and controlling the finances, the opposite is true. Said Mrs Fukawo, 'At the end of the week the majority of husbands hand the whole of their pay packet to the wife, and she then hands them back their allowance. Indeed,' she said, 'in Japanese humour the equivalent of the British "mother-in-law" joke is the Japanese "mean wife who keeps her husband short of pocket money" joke.'

It was, incidentally, after this programme that Fuyoko, our Japanese researcher, told us what must be the definitive story about Japanese husbands. She said, 'Like most Japanese husbands, my old man's pet name for me is "Oi".' She went on, 'Morning to night he just says, "Oi, breakfast. Oi, lunch. Oi, the paper. Oi, a beer." '

My last two guests were the Commercial Counsellor at the British Embassy in Tokyo, Merrick Baker-Bates, and the Chairman of the British Chamber of Commerce, Norman McCloud. I asked Merrick whether the Japanese really were, as they were often portrayed, supermen, conquering all before them. Said Merrick, 'No they are not, they've had a lot of successes but they've also had their difficulties. There are, in this market, a good many niches which British exporters could fill. The name of the game is to find those niches, and we can help them.'

163

Norman McCloud spoke up. He said, 'Japan is a desperately poor country when it comes to energy, in that every ton of oil has to be shipped in, so they have a great weakness there. We must think harder to find the niches of which Merrick has spoken.' He slipped into a football comparison, 'If you're playing a very, very good team, you don't just pack the goal and defend. That isn't a goal-scoring, winning strategy. Defence, yes, but you must also think your way through to attack.'

We had just a couple of minutes left and I wanted a final comment from each of my two British guests. Merrick went first with a comparison of the interest shown by British companies in Japan and China. He said, 'Recently we had an energy-saving seminar here which attracted eight British companies. I couldn't help remembering that a couple of years ago, 350 companies went to China on exactly the same theme. Nobody can tell me that the prospects for British exports to Japan in that field aren't better than they are to China, given the immense attention to energy-saving here.'

The final word came from Norman. I asked him what he had found to be his biggest problem when he came to live and work in Japan. He said, 'My biggest problem was the language. I was desperately enthusiastic to learn it so I went to a shop and bought a book called, *Japanese in Six Months*. I then saw, *Japanese in Three Months* followed by, *Japanese in Three Weeks*. And when I saw *Instant Japanese*, I got really excited. Six years later I'm still trying to make myself understood by taxi drivers!' He went on, 'In Japan last year Government and Industry got together and produced what they called "A vision for the eighties", spelling out where Japan is going in the next ten years. That is what we should be doing in Britain. The 'C.B.I., Government, unions and banks should get together and think more positively. Study the Japanese vision, and then decide what the counter-attack is going to be.'

It was 8 p.m. in Tokyo, 12 noon in London, and our three-day stint was over. It was almost time to say goodbye to our hosts, and new-found friends, at NHK.

We had laid on a buffet-type meal for them, and then it really was goodbye. There was a formal speech on behalf of

NHK, and Harry made a brief, formal speech on behalf of the BBC. Then, just when the whole thing looked like getting a bit stuffy, I made a speech in excruciating Japanese, written out phonetically for me by Fuyoko, which everyone agreed was the funniest thing that had happened all week!

It was a very pleasant end to what for me, and I hope for our listeners, had been a fascinating trip.

In June, I once again went to Buckingham Palace to interview H.R.H. Prince Philip, The Duke of Edinburgh. It was an interview which contained one unfortunate Royal reference to leisure and unemployment. The remark, I am certain, was not meant to carry the inference which it seemed to, as the Palace pointed out in an apology later in the day. I am sure that the Duke of Edinburgh was simply suggesting how to respond to leisure and use it, whether leisure brought about by unemployment, or new technology. However, in all the press fury which followed, the *Guardian* carried a rather neat defence of Prince Philip. In its leading article of 13 June, it opened with: 'What the Duke of Edinburgh said to Jimmy Young about the jobless has been universally condemned, not least, after the event, by Prince Philip himself.' It listed various incomparably worse Royal indiscretions of the past, naming Charles II, George IV, and James I. The leader went on, 'The fact that, according to the admittedly imperfect records of the time, there was no "Jimmy Young Show" to record their various indiscretions does not necessarily prove that no indiscretions took place.'

It was reunion day on the programme on 26 June. Founder member of the 'JY Prog', now Managing Director BBC External Services, Douglas Muggeridge came in to talk about the Government's proposed cut backs in funding, some three million pounds. Compared with the massive amounts of money successive Governments had been prepared to pour into enterprises like British Leyland, it seemed a fiddling little amount. And when Douglas proceeded to list the areas in which, because of this minute saving, the Government would lose the ability to put across the British point of view it seemed an absolutely crazy thing to do.

On 1 July Opposition Leader, Michael Foot, came on to warn the 'infantile Left in the Labour Party that they would have to be dealt with'. He somewhat spoiled the hard line a moment later, however, by saying that he remained opposed to the idea of expelling anyone from the party, and believed it could all be dealt with by persuasion. I expressed the thought that many people, including some in the Labour Party, would doubt that.

The real fireworks arrived on Friday 3 July in the shape of former Conservative Prime Minister, Mr Edward Heath. Ted had been ill and out of the limelight for a while. He certainly made up for lost time as he laid about him on the Prog.

As the front page of *The Times* said the following day, 'In another astonishing outburst against the Government's approach on many issues, Mr Edward Heath continued his onslaught yesterday by telling Mrs Thatcher, in the bluntest language, that neither she, nor anyone else in the Conservative Party, would stop him from speaking out.'

At various times during the interview he called the Thatcher Government's political style and strategy 'childish', 'stupid', 'ridiculous'. He told me that, in his experience, businessmen found the Government economic policy incomprehensible. They were baffled by its contradictions. In a telling phrase, and in ringing tones, he declared, 'I am not going to be intimidated by anybody, whether it be by the Press, or the battling brigadiers who send me stinking letters. I do not mind. There is no need to write. I am going to tell the country plain home-truths which the great majority of people recognize.

'I am not going to stop. I shall not be stopped in the House. I shall not be stopped by anybody in No.10. I shall go on doing it.'

I again asked him whether he might quit the Conservative Party and join the Social Democrats. Said he, 'I have absolutely no intention of getting out.' It was one of the strongest most outspoken interviews I had ever heard on the programme. Beset by unemployment, a troubled economy, and rioting in the streets, I wondered what Mrs Thatcher would make of it all.

Late in 1981 I talked on the programme with the Archbishop of Canterbury's special adviser, Terry Waite. We were discussing the fate of Miss Jean Waddell, Dr John Coleman and his wife Andrea, and Andrew Pyke, all detained in prison in Iran.

Terry was trying to negotiate their release and, in the case of the first three seemed to be making good progress, indeed they were released shortly after we talked. However, in the case of Andrew Pyke he seemed to be getting nowhere.

The Ayatollah Khomeni's regime had accused Andrew of spying, although those accusations had been dropped. Instead Andrew was now accused of 'financial irregularities' and, despite his protests of innocence, was still held prisoner, without even the prospect of being brought to trial.

Our listeners were interested, concerned, and sympathetic. However, exactly how sympathetic we were not to discover until the New Year.

On Wednesday 27 January 1982, the JY team was busy opening and sorting our, as always, huge quantity of mail. The address at the head of one letter, reproduced overleaf, read Ghezel Hesar Prison, Karaj, R.I. Iran. From there, the letter had been sent by the incarcerated, still untried Andrew Pyke.

It was with great joy that I included Andrew's message in the programme. Even as I was reading it I was made aware yet again not of the 'power' of the programme, as journalists sometimes refer to it, but of the brightness, intelligence and warmth of the people who listen to it and are such an important part of it. When they feel something needs doing they don't just sit there, they get up and do something about it.

Let's face it, any nation that can chip in one-and-a-quarter million pounds for handicapped children on a purely local Telethon and send, completely unsolicited, 10,000 Christmas cards to a total stranger in an Iranian gaol, can't be all bad.

Ghezel Hesar prison,
Karaj,
R.I. Iran

12th January, 1982

Dear Mr. Young — A request for your assistance, if
I may? My somewhat unusual circumstances have
resulted in my being inundated with thousands of
Christmas cards and letters of encouragement from all
over the U.K. 99.9% of these are from people who
are strangers to me, and I have no way to thank
them all, other than through you. If you are able,
please say I have been overwhelmed, cheered and
strengthened enormously by the flood of kindness and
goodwill I've received. In a situation such as mine,
you have no idea what one Christmas card can mean,
let alone thousands! My gratitude to everyone is
endless. I'm glad to say I'm in pretty good shape
here; I truly have no complaints regarding my present
living conditions — yet naturally am eager to be home,
which I hope will not be long forthcoming. My
treatment by the revolutionary authorities has always
been good and courteous, which is surely confirmed by
the fact that they have authorised the mailing of
this, and other letters. With thanks for your anticipated
assistance, and regards,

Andrew Pyke

PS - why not play a quick
blast of something that makes you smile?

14 - Wogan!!

I'm often asked about the special relationship which exists between myself and the leprechaun from Limerick, Terence Wogan.

Our names were first linked way back in 1969. It was in that year, and using my broad shoulders as a launching pad, that he first projected his portly personage towards stellar stardom. Yes, I'm afraid I must own up. The whole tragic story is all my fault.

It's my fault that you have to put up with his esoteric (his pet word, though he knows not what it means) chat, at a time of day when the human mind is in no condition to take it.

It's my fault that you're lumbered with those pregnant pauses when the record ends and it takes him ten seconds to remember that he's supposed to say something.

It's my fault that, most of the time you end up hearing the wrong side of the record anyway, because the old *twit* (his name for himself, not mine) can't read very well, and has great difficulty in telling the 'A' side from the 'B' side.

It's my fault that you suffered the hell of 'Blankety Blank'.

Yet, it all seemed so innocent at the time. All that happened, those many years ago, was that I took a couple of weeks holiday. Seems perfectly reasonable, doesn't it? Surely there's nothing wrong in that. Yet look at the result.

The Beeb decided to hire Wogan as a two-week holiday replacement for me and, thirteen years later, we're still stuck with him. Too late I realized what I had done. Never should I have succumbed to the sirens calling me to the fleshpots of the South of France. I should have put on my headphones, turned up the volume and drowned out their beguiling voices. I should have chained myself to the microphone, and thus saved us all from the dreadful fate which has befallen us.

When my own programme began at 11.30 a.m. it wasn't so bad. At least then I had the protection of a ninety-minute gap between us. No, it was when I moved to the 10 o'clock slot that, in a single moment of madness, I doomed myself to daily morning torture for the rest of my contractual life.

It happened on the very first morning. At about a quarter past nine I walked, all unsuspectingly, into Studio Continuity 'D'. From behind my head – yes he really does, as he often tells you, spend his mornings looking at the back of my head, came the dulcet Irish tones. 'Hello, Jimbo,' he cried, 'why don't you pop into my studio a little later on, say at about a quarter to ten, and trail what you're going to be doing in your programme between 10 and 12?'

Naïve fool that I am, I thought; what a kindly Irish gentleman he is to be sure, and I accepted. Had I known him then as well as I know him now I would also have known that kindliness was far from being the prime motivating factor behind his thinking. Survival, more likely. It didn't take me long to find out that, by the time he's been on the air for two hours he has totally run out of things to say. What is more, his audience are absolutely bored out of their skulls, and are desperate for someone charming, intelligent, talented and witty, to pop in and pep things up a bit. Need I say more?

What I had *not* bargained for, of course, was that, in very short order he would succeed in dragging me down to his level. That, however, I fear, is what happened. Within a week we were discussing suspender belts. During week two, in one of those moments that flash through the mind like a nightmare, he raised the question of the merits of cami-knickers as opposed to knickers with tight gussets. By week three, we were heavily into the *Directoire* variety. Almost literally. Our studios were full of them as listeners sent them in by the hundreds!

I was surprised, as I turned up at the studio each morning,

to see him still sitting there. I quite thought that Lord Reith would have struck him down personally with a thunderbolt. I needn't have worried. The luck of the Irish prevailed, as I might have known it would. The listeners loved it. The bosses loved it. The Board of Governors loved it. As I was to discover one morning in 1979, even Her Majesty The Queen loved it. Emboldened by it all, Wogan daily plunges me ever further into dangerous, and often uncharted, waters.

As I write this we have not yet been fired. By the time the book is published, who knows?

15 - Summing Up

Writing this book has been a particularly enjoyable, and interesting, exercise for me. It has sent me back to my personal notes and reading those has been like living the past nine years over again, in slow motion. With some surprising results.

I never would have believed, for instance, that the programme could have changed as much as it has since 1973. Yet, nine years ago, we were still in the age of the JY catchphrase: 'Orft we jolly well go', 'This is what you do', 'Kiddley-winkles'. . . . Today they have all gone. Not because we had a conference and decided that they should but as the programme changed and developed they seemed not to fit comfortably any more.

Nine years ago Raymondo was still shouting a daily 'What's The Recipe Today, Jim?' Now, no Raymondo and no recipe.

It is almost as though the programme and its audience have matured and developed together, retaining the best of the old programme while reacting to new circumstances and ideas.

Back in 1973 we were still thought of as a 'housewives' programme', which of course we are proud to be. However, over the years, we have found that we get an ever increasing number of letters, and telephone calls from men, especially professional men: doctors, lawyers, M.P.s and so on.

With the help and involvement of our listeners, we have evolved into a much broader-based, thought-provoking programme, covering a much wider spectrum of life. For many

172

more people than nine years ago, at home and at work, we provide an extra window on the world.

It has taken a lot of hard work and things have often not been easy. But then, few worthwhile things are. The programme has always taken up eighty per cent or more of my time. During the past year, when I've been working on this book it has taken up a hundred per cent. However, by nature I am a home-loving person so, sitting at my desk in the evenings pounding a typewriter is not a hardship for me. Especially when the atmosphere at home is happy, as it now is.

Happiness at home had always seemed to elude me, in spite of having several really smashing ladies pass in and out of my life. Clearly a lot of the trouble was with me. I had not yet found the lady who could change me and do it so subtly that I didn't even realize it was happening. Now my friends tell me that I am a different person. There is a peace and tranquillity about my life which was never there before and Alicia is the person who, quietly, brought about the change. What is it the song says? 'When he fancies he is past love, it is then he meets his last love, and he loves her as he's never loved before.'

I will end with an anecdote. I include it for aspiring broadcasters, feeling frustrated in their efforts to get started. It may help them to feel marginally less suicidal.

In October 1981 I was appearing on the 'Michael Parkinson Show' on BBC Television. Michael asked me whether I had found things difficult at the beginning of my career.

I replied that I auditioned for, and was turned down by, just about everyone in show business. I added that one eminent agent, a lovely lady named Lillian Aza, had personally turned me down on three separate occasions.

The day after the 'Parkinson Show' my telephone rang. It was Lillian, now in semi-retirement. She told me how much she had enjoyed seeing me again and how, as I was telling the story of my rejection slips, memories of 1949 came back to her.

She said, 'I shall never forget the letter I received from the BBC after I sent you to audition for them. It read, "Dear Mrs Aza, we regret to have to inform you that, in our opinion, Mr Young will never be broadcasting material."

Index

Numbers in *italics* refer to illustrations.
(Jimmy Young has not been included in the index.)